10/15

 D0535306

KNiTTiNG CLOTHES KiDS LOVE

**Creative Publishing
international**

Copyright © 2013 Creative Publishing international, Inc.

All rights reserved. No part of this work covered by the copyrights hereon may
be reproduced or used in any form or by any means—graphic, electronic, or
mechanical, including photocopying, recording, taping of information on stor-
age and retrieval systems—without the written permission of the publisher.

Due to differing conditions, materials, and skill levels, the publisher and vari-
ous manufacturers disclaim any liability for unsatisfactory results or injury due to
improper use of tools, materials, or information in this publication.

First published in the United States of America by
Creative Publishing international, Inc., a member of
Quayside Publishing Group
400 First Avenue North
Suite 300
Minneapolis, MN 55401
1-800-328-3895
www.creativepub.com

ISBN: 978-1-58923-675-2

10 9 8 7 6 5 4 3 2 1

Library of Congress Cataloging-in-Publication Data available

Technical Editor: Tana Pageler
Copy Editor: Kari Cornell
Proofreader: India Tresselt
Book Design: Kathie Alexander
Cover Design: Creative Publishing International
Page Layout: Kathie Alexander
Illustrations: Kate Oates
Photographs: Nancy J. S. Langdon

Printed in China

KNiTTiNG CLOTHES KiDS LOVE

COLORFUL ACCESSORIES FOR HEADS, SHOULDERS, KNEES, HANDS, TOES

KATE OATES

PHOTOGRAPHY BY NANCY J. S. LANGDON

NORTHERN PLAINS
PUBLIC LIBRARY
Ault, Colorado

✭ Contents

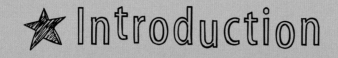

★ Introduction

What's the best thing about knitting for children? There are no rules. Kids can rock quirky color combinations, asymmetry, "clashing" patterns, you name it! And they love it. Don't think for one minute boys aren't included in this analysis. I know from personal experience that boys can be just as excited as girls about wearing intriguing clothes. This book is full of super-fun accessories, each with many options to make it unique.

Knitting Clothes Kids Love: Heads, Shoulders, Knees, Hands, Toes is organized into six sections based on where the knit is worn. I start with the head then move to shoulders, knees, hands, and toes. I've included conventional items, like hats and scarves and socks, but also more adventurous accessories, like hair embellishments, a backpack, and bracelets. Chapter one includes a sizing overview and a two-part stitch dictionary, allowing you to really mix and match the colors and stitch patterns to best suit the exceptional recipient. I encourage you to think of each sample as a jumping-off point, rather than a pattern to follow step-by-step.

Chapter 1

Knitting for Kids

Gauge

I've provided a gauge for every pattern. There are a couple of items where the gauge is more of a suggestion than a necessity, and you'll see that noted. Otherwise, you should know that all sizing is based on the gauge. Unfortunately, if your knitting doesn't match the gauge provided, it's impossible to determine how it will fit.

To avoid this, I urge you to take the time to make a gauge swatch and block it. If you skip the swatching and blocking step and go straight to knitting, you might have some unexpected (and unhappy) results. Knit a swatch that is at least 5 inches square and measure 4 inches worth of stitches, up and down, without including any selvedge edge in the measurement. Pay attention to the stitch pattern called for in the swatch and watch your needle size when more than one is called for in the pattern. Keep in mind that all needle sizes required to obtain the gauge may vary from knitter to knitter. The needle sizes provided are those I used, but every knitter is different. If the pattern calls for more than one needle size, make note of how many sizes are between those suggested and make these same accommodations to your needle sizes according to your gauge. Finally, once you've bound off your swatch, be sure to block it. Depending on the fiber content, your gauge might actually change during blocking.

Fit

Scattered throughout the book are some great accessories that are designed to be one-size-fits-all! Hooray! If you're knitting one of these patterns, you don't have to give any thought as to how it will fit.

But most of the patterns do include at least a few sizes. Here's a general guideline:

Toddler: this size should work for kids between the ages of 2 and somewhere between 4 and 6.

Child: this size picks up where toddler leaves off, and goes up to ages 10 through 12.

Teen: I recommend this size for kids ages 13 and up; many of these would work for adults too!

Because kids come in all shapes and sizes, each pattern also includes relevant measurement notation for each size. This will be especially helpful if the child seems to be between sizes. For each pattern, check the Pattern Notes to find out the size of the sample pictured and to learn more about how the garment is expected to fit, also known as the suggested "ease" of the garment.

Ease

The term "ease" refers to how snugly or loosely the finished garment should fit. If an item is sized with negative ease, this means the finished knit should be smaller than the actual measurement of the child. Conversely, if an item is sized with positive ease, it should be larger. If an item has no ease this means it should have a fit that is very close or the same as the wearer's actual measurement.

Ease can also be used as a tool to help make a knit seem to grow with a child, or last a bit longer. For example, if I suggest 2 inches of negative ease but the provided measurements give a choice of either 1 or 3 inches of negative ease, I suggest working the larger size, since kids are always growing!

Abbreviations

" :	inch(es)
[ ] :	rep instructions between brackets as many times as indicated
BO:	bind off
CO:	cast on
DPN(s):	double pointed needle(s)
K, k:	knit
LH:	left hand
mm:	millimeter
P, p:	purl
Pat:	pattern
PM:	place marker
Rep:	repeat
Rem:	remaining
Rev St st:	reverse stockinette stitch; purl all sts on the right side, knit all sts on the wrong side
RH:	right hand
RS:	right side
Sl:	slip
SM:	slip marker
St st:	stockinette stitch; knit all sts on the right side, purl all sts on the wrong side
St(s):	stitch(es)
WS:	wrong side
WYIF:	with yarn in front

Increases

Kf&b:	knit into the front and back of the same stitch
Kf&b&f:	knit into the front and back and front of the same stitch
M1:	make 1 st
M1L:	make 1 left-leaning st
M1R:	make 1 right-leaning st
YO:	yarn over
YFON:	yarn forward over needle

Decreases

K2tog:	knit two sts together
P2tog:	purl two sts together
Ssk:	slip 2 sts knitwise, knit these 2 sts together

Cabling

X2:	Crossover: slip 1 st to cable needle and hold to front, k1, k1 from cable needle
T3B:	slip 1 st to cable needle and hold to back, k2, p1 from cable needle
T3F:	slip 2 sts to cable needle and hold to front, p1, k2 from cable needle
C4B:	slip 2 sts to cable needle and hold to back, k2, k2 from cable needle
C4F:	slip 2 sts to cable needle and hold to front, k2, k2 from cable needle
T4B:	slip 2 sts to cable needle and hold to back, k2, p2 from cable needle
T4F:	slip 2 sts to cable needle and hold to front, p2, k2 from cable needle
C6B:	slip 3 sts to cable needle and hold to back, k3, k3 from cable needle
C6F:	slip 3 sts to cable needle and hold to front, k3, k3 from cable needle
C12B:	slip 6 sts to cable needle and hold to back, k6, k6 from cable needle
C12F:	slip 6 sts to cable needle and hold to front, k6, k6 from cable needle

Techniques

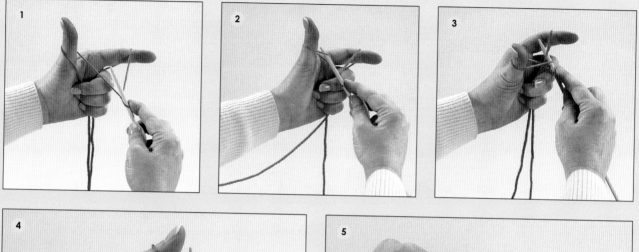

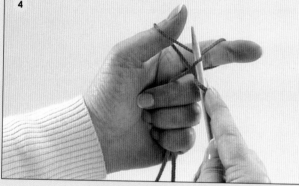

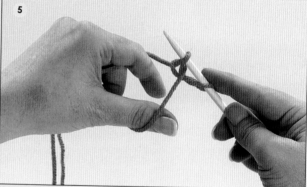

Long Tail Cast-On

Make a slipknot on the needle and hold the needle in your right hand. Put the thumb and index finger of your left hand between the tail and working yarn, with the tail around your thumb and the working yarn around your index finger.

1 Use the other fingers of your left hand to hold both strands snugly against your left palm.

2 Insert the needle upward through the loop on your thumb.

3 Pivot the needle to the right and go over and under the yarn on your index finger, picking up a loop.

4 Pull the loop back down through the thumb loop.

5 Let your thumb drop out of the loop and reinsert it. Spread your fingers to snug up the new stitch on the needle.

Repeat the steps for each stitch.

Cable Cast-On

Other cast-on methods are used in specific situations. The cable cast-on is useful if you need to add stitches to your knitting after you've already worked several rows or rounds. Insert the right needle into the space between the last two stitches on your left needle.

1 Wrap the yarn around your needle and pull a loop through.

2 Put this loop back on your left needle.

3 You've just cast on one stitch. Continue in this manner, adding as many stitches as are called for in the pattern.

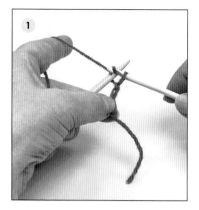

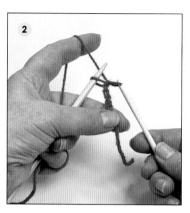

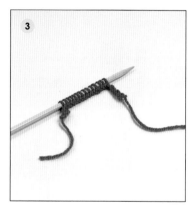

Provisional Cast-On

This method allows you to remove the cast-on row later, leaving a row of "live" stitches that can be placed on a needle and knitted in the opposite direction. This cast-on technique has many uses, and many patterns call for it. There are also several ways to achieve a provisional cast-on. My favorite is to use a crochet hook to put the stitches on the needle. It is quite easy to do, and easy to remove the provisional yarn when done.

1 With a contrasting yarn, make a slip knot then chain 2 or 3 stitches with crochet hook. Hold a knitting needle in your left hand, over the working yarn that is coming from the crochet hook in your right hand. Take the hook over the needle, wrap the yarn over the hook, and pull it through the loop on the hook, making a chain.

2 Reposition the working yarn under the needle, and make another stitch over the needle. Continue until you have made the required number of stitches.

3 Chain two or three stitches with just the crochet hook, cut the yarn, and pull the end through. Make a knot in the beginning tail, so that you know to pull the end without the knot when it comes time to unravel the provisional cast-on.

4 Drop the contrast yarn and, starting with the first row, knit the stitches with your project yarn. When you are ready to knit from the cast-on edge, release the stitches of the contrast yarn and pick up the live stitches with your knitting needle.

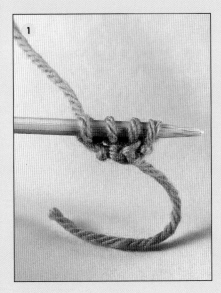

Bind Off

Finishing the last row or round of a knitted project so that it will not unravel is called binding off. In the conventional method of binding off, usually done from the right side, you knit the first two stitches, then, using your left needle, lift the second stitch on the right needle up and over the stitch that you've just knit, allowing the second stitch to drop off the tip of the right needle. One stitch is bound off. Repeat this, one stitch at a time, until all stitches are bound off. Use this method whenever a pattern instructs you to bind off all stitches.

If the pattern tells you to bind off in pattern, you knit or purl each stitch following the stitch pattern that has been established, before binding it off.

When binding off in a cable pattern, it is a good idea to bind off just after a twist row to keep the stitches from stretching.

Binding off can sometimes make the edge too tight. To prevent this, bind off with a needle at least two sizes larger than you used for knitting the project.

I-cord

Cast on or pick up the required number of stitches on a double-pointed needle. Knit the stitches with another double-pointed needle, but don't turn the work.

1 Slide the stitches to the opposite end of the needle.

2 Pull the working yarn tight across the back of the stitches and knit another row.

3 Repeat this many times, forming a tiny knitted tube. To keep the stitches looking uniform, tug on the tube every few rows.

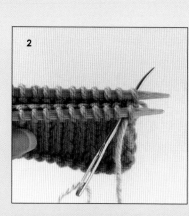

Grafting/Kitchener Stitch

Kitchener stitch, also known as grafting, is the seaming method of choice when you need to join a row of live stitches to a second row of live stitches. It produces a seam that's virtually undetectable. To help demonstrate the steps, a contrasting yarn has been used in the photos. Cut the working yarn, leaving a tail about 18˝ (46 cm) long. Leave the stitches on the needles; there should be the same number of stitches on each. Hold the needles side-by-side in the left hand, with the right side facing up. Slide the stitches toward the needle tips.

1 Arrange so that the working yarn is coming from the first stitch on the back needle. Thread the yarn tail on a yarn needle. Draw the yarn through the first stitch on the front needle as if to purl, and leave the stitch on the needle.

2 Keeping the yarn under the needles, draw the yarn through the first stitch on the back needle as if to knit, and leave the stitch on the needle.

3 * Draw the yarn through the first stitch on the front needle as if to knit, and slip the stitch off the needle. Draw the yarn through the next stitch on the front needle as if to purl, and leave the stitch on the needle.

4 Draw the yarn through the first stitch on the back needle as if to purl, and slip the stitch off the needle. Draw the yarn through the next stitch on the back needle as if to knit, and leave the stitch on the needle.

5 Repeat from * until all but the last two stitches have been worked off the needles. Insert the tapestry needle knitwise into the stitch on the front needle, and purlwise into the stitch on the back needle, slipping both stitches off their respective needles. Stretch out your seam or use the tip of a needle to adjust stitches a bit and even out the tension in the yarn

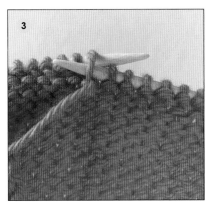

One-row Buttonhole

Starting at buttonhole, WYIF, sl 1 st. Move yarn to back. *Sl 1 st, pass first sl st over second and off needle; repeat from * to BO desired number of sts. Sl last st on RH needle back to LH needle. Turn. Cable CO the number of sts that were BO. CO one additional st, but before transferring new st to LH needle, bring yarn to front between new st and first st on LH needle. Turn. Sl 1 st, pass first st over second and off needle to close buttonhole.

W&T

1 Wrap and turn for short row shaping. When next st is to be knit: After working last st, with yarn in back sl next st purlwise onto RH needle.

2 Move yarn to front then sl st back onto LH needle.

3 Turn and work back as directed

Jeny's Surprisingly Stretchy Bind-Off

Each stitch will be balanced with a yarn over before it is bound off. When working a knit stitch: YFON, k1, sl YO over knit st. When working a purl st: YO, p1, sl YO over purl st. To bind off: Work the first two stitches, pass right stitch over left and off needle, [work next stitch, pass right stitch over left and off needle] until 1 st rem. Cut yarn, weave through rem st and secure.

Pom-poms

Feel free to use your own pom-pom making tool, or make a different size pom-pom! Here are some directions in case you need a little guidance. Cut two circles the size of the desired pom-pom from a piece of cardboard. Cut a ½-inch hole in the center of both circles. Thread a tapestry needle with a long length of yarn. Wrap yarn around the outside edge of the cardboard circle, passing it through the center hole each time. When the entire outside edge of the circle is covered with yarn, slide a scissors between the two cardboard circles and cut the yarn along the outside edge. Cut another 6-inch piece of yarn and slide it between the cardboard circles, wrapping it twice around the middle of your bundle, tie tightly and double knot (at least). Remove cardboard circles. Voila! Now just use your scissors to trim up and shape the pom-pom.

Single Crochet

Make slip knot and place on crochet hook. *Insert hook into an edge stitch, yarn over hook, and draw a loop through stitch, yarn over hook, then draw it through both loops on hook. Rep from * for single crochet.

I-cord Bind-Off

Hold work with RS facing, ready to BO. CO 3 sts. *K2, ssk (last I-cord st with next st of edge being bound off). Sl 3 sts now on DPN back to LH needle. Repeat from * for bind-off.

Stitch Dictionary Part 1: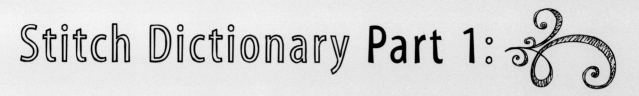

Colorwork and Motif Options

Incorporating color into your knits adds whimsy and cheer. This "dictionary" includes all of the colorwork and motif options used throughout the book. All stranded colorwork in this book is worked in stockinette stitch—which means that stitches are knit on the right side and purled on the wrong side. When working in the round, stitches are knit only. With some careful consideration, you can substitute many of these patterns to make different pieces go together better, or just to change them up. Account for the following factors when you make substitutions.

Stitch Repeat

If a piece is being worked in the round, you will need to make sure that the stitch repeat of the pattern fits evenly into the number of stitches within the garment. If it does not fit, you will need to modify the stitch pattern itself or the number of stitches in the garment. For example, the larger Wavy Stripe Pattern is worked over a multiple of 12 stitches. Suppose you wanted to use it for the Toddler size of the Funky Fair Isle Socks pattern. This size is worked over 32 stitches total. Because 32 cannot be divided evenly by 12, you'll need to adjust the Wavy Stripe Pattern to a multiple that is divisible by 8, 4, or 2. You might choose to go with another pattern worked over one of these multiples. Or, you could increase by 4 stitches in the leg of the sock in order to get to 36, which is divisible by 12. If you were working the Teen size of this same pattern, which has 48 stitches total, the Wavy Stripe Pattern would work just fine, as 48 does divide evenly by 12. In this case the stitch pattern could be used without adjustment. If all this sounds too complicated for you, remember only this: substitute stitch patterns that divide evenly into your project stitch count.

If a piece is being worked flat, back and forth, it is a little easier to make substitutions because it is not necessarily important for exact repeats to be completed. Instead there can be partial repeats on the edges of the knit. Substitute at will, just remember how many extra stitches there are on the edge so that your pattern does not shift back and forth.

Stranding

Any knitting motif in which two or more colors are repeated across a row and the unused colors are gently carried on the wrong side of the work is called stranded colorwork. The strands in the back create an extra layer of fabric. There are a few things to be mindful of if you are substituting a stranded stitch pattern into a design that does not initially include this style of knitting. First, be aware that your gauge can change when you are knitting stranded colorwork. If the majority of the piece will feature stranded colorwork, always do your gauge swatch in this type of pattern. Second, sizing is done a little bit differently with a stranded design. The extra layer of yarn in the back makes the fabric less elastic, so adjustments must be made in the overall ease of the garment. For example, if a hat is designed with 2 inches of negative ease when it is to be worked without stranding, I might adjust and change that negative ease to only 1 inch when adding a stranded colorwork pattern. This would mean making an actual change in stitch count, or, perhaps following the next larger size but using length measurements for the original size. If all this sounds too complicated for you, remember only this: substitute stranded stitch patterns for other stranded stitch patterns and avoid adding stranding to non-stranded designs.

The Patterns

Each pattern is written either in "Rounds" or "Rows," depending on whether the corresponding design was worked in the round or back and forth. Most patterns in this book are meant to be knitted in the round, but can be knit flat provided that you adjust for knits and purls on the right and wrong sides. However, remember that if you are adjusting an in-the-round pattern to working back and forth, pick a color pattern in which the one color does not get abandoned at the end of a row, only to be needed again on the other side. Otherwise, you'll be forced to cut yarn all over the place, leaving lots of ends to weave in.

The easiest way to add color is by using stripes. Horizontal stripes can be worked over any multiple of stitches because there is only one color used in any given row!

2-Row Even Stripes

Rows 1-2: Work in A.
Rows 3-4: Work in B.

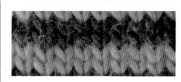

Uneven Stripes

Rounds 1-2: Work in A.
Round 3: Work in B.
Rounds 4-5: Work in A.
Rounds 6–8: Work in B.

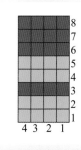

Kooky Stripes

Rounds 1-2: Work in A.
Round 3: Work in B.
Rounds 4–6: Work in C.
Round 7: Work in A.
Rounds 8-9: Work in B.
Round 10: Work in C.

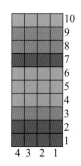

Vertical Stripes (worked over an even number of sts)

All Rounds: *With A, k1, with B, k1; rep from * around.

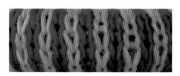

Going Left (worked over a multiple of 4 sts)

Round 1: *With A, k2, with B, k2; rep from * to end.
Round 2: *With B, k1, with A, k2, with B, k1; rep from * to end.
Round 3: *With B, k2, with A, k2; rep from * to end.
Round 4: *With A, k1, with B, k2, with A, k1; rep from * to end.

Going Right (worked over a multiple of 4 sts)

Round 1: *With A, k2, with B, k2; rep from * to end.
Round 2: *With A, k1, with B, k2, with A, k1; rep from * to end.
Round 3: *With B, k2, with A, k2; rep from * to end.
Round 4: *With B, k1, with A, k2, with B, k1; rep from * to end.

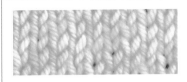

Skinny Spiral (worked over a multiple of 4 sts)

Round 1: *With A, k3, with B, k1; rep from * to end.
Round 2: *With A, k2, with B, k1, with A, k1; rep from * to end.
Round 3: *With A, k1, with B, k1, with A, k2; rep from * to end.
Round 4: *With B, k1, with A, k3; rep from * to end.

Spiral (worked over a multiple of 8 sts)

Round 1: *With B, k4, with A, k4; rep from * to end.
Round 2: *With B, k3, with A, k4, with B, k1; rep from * to end.
Round 3: *With B, k2, with A, k4, with B, k2; rep from * to end.
Round 4: *With B, k1, with A, k4, with B, k3; rep from * to end.
Round 5: *With A, k4, with B, k4; rep from * to end.
Round 6: *With A, k3, with B, k4, with A, k1; rep from * to end.
Round 7: *With A, k2, with B, k4, with A, k2; rep from * to end.
Round 8: *With A, k1, with B, k4, with A, k3; rep from * to end.

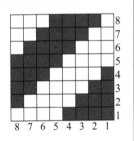

Choppy Stripes (worked over a multiple of 6 sts)

Row 1 (RS): With A, *k2tog twice, kf&b twice
rep from * to end.
Row 2: With A, purl.
Row 3: With B, *k2tog twice, kf&b twice; rep from * to end.
Row 4: With B, purl.

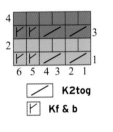

◺ K2tog
◹ Kf & b

Wavy Stripes (worked over a multiple of 12 sts)

Round 1: With A, knit.
Round 2: *K2tog 4 times, kf&b 4 times; rep from * to end.
Round 3: Knit.
Round 4-6: With B, repeat Rounds 1–3.

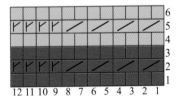
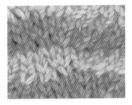

◺ K2tog
◹ Kf & b

Little Zigzag (worked over an even number of sts)

Rounds 1-2: With A, knit.
Round 3: *With A, k1, with B, k1; rep from * to end.
Round 4: *With B, k1, with A, k1; rep from * to end.

Medium Zigzag (worked over a multiple of 4 sts)

Round 1: *With A, k3, with B, k1; rep from * to end.
Round 2: *With B, k1, with A, k1, with B, k2; rep from * to end.
Round 3: *With B, k3, with A, k1; rep from * to end.
Round 4: *With A, k1, with B, k1, with A, k2; rep from * to end.

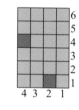

Bitty Dots (worked over a multiple of 4 sts)

Round 1: *With A, k1, with B, k1, with A, k2; rep from * around.
Rounds 2-3: With A, knit.
Round 4: *With A, k3, with B, k1; rep from * around.
Round 5-6: With A, knit.

Polka Dots (worked over a multiple of 8 sts)

Round 1: With A, knit.
Round 2: *With A, k2, with B, k3, with A, k3; rep from * to end.
Round 3: *With A, k1, with B, k5, with A, k2; rep from * to end.
Rounds 4–6: *With B, k7, with A, k1; rep from * to end.
Round 7: *With A, k1, with B, k5, with A, k2; rep from * to end.
Round 8: *With A, k2, with B, k3, with A, k3; rep from * to end.
Rounds 9-10: With A, knit.
Round 11: *With B, k1, with A, k5, with B, k2; rep from * to end.
Round 12: *With B, k2, with A, k3, with B, k3; rep from * to end.
Rounds 13-15: *With B, k3, with A, k1, with B, k4;
rep from * to end.
Round 16: *With B, k2, with A, k3, with B, k3; rep from * to end.
Round 17: *With B, k1, with A, k5, with B, k2; rep from * to end.
Round 18: With A, knit.

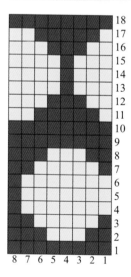

Stripe & Dot (worked over an even number of sts)

Round 1: With A, knit.
Round 2: With B, knit.
Round 3: *With B, k1, with C, k1; rep from * to end.
Round 4: With B, knit.
Round 5: With A, knit.
Round 6: With C, knit.
Round 7: *With C, k1, with B, k1; rep from * to end.
Round 8: With C, knit.

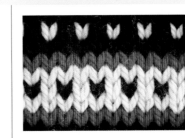

Stripe & Block (worked over a multiple of 4 sts)

Round 1: With A, knit.
Rounds 2–4: *With B, k2, with C, k2; rep from * to end.
Round 5: With D, knit.

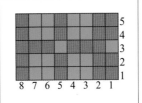

Flower & Dot (worked over a multiple of 8 sts)

Rounds 1-2: *With A, k2, [with B, k2, with A, k1] twice; rep from * to end.
Round 3: *With B, k1, with A, k3; rep from * to end.
Rounds 4-5: *With A, k2, [with B, k2, with A, k1] twice; rep from * to end.
If working this pattern alone as a repeat, consider adding Round 6, knit in A.

Ticking (worked over an even number of sts)

Round 1: *With A, k1, with B, k1; rep from * to end.
Round 2: With A, knit.
Round 3: *With B, k1, with A, k1; rep from * to end.
If working this pattern alone as a repeat, consider adding Round 4, knit in B.

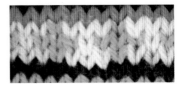

Cross (worked over a multiple of 4 sts)

Round 1: *With A, k2, with B, k1, with A, k1; rep from * to end.
Round 2: *With A, k1, with B, k3; rep from * to end.
Round 3: *With A, k2, with B, k1, with A, k1; rep from * to end.
If working this pattern alone as a repeat, consider adding Round 4, knit in A.

Open Diamond (worked over a multiple of 4 sts)

Round 1: *With A, k1, with B, k1, with A, k2; rep from * to end.
Round 2: *With B, k3, with A, k1; rep from * to end.
Round 3: *With B, k1, with A, k1, with B, k2; rep from * to end.
Round 4: *With B, k3, with A, k1; rep from * to end.
Round 5: *With A, k1, with B, k1, with A, k2; rep from * to end.
If working this pattern alone as a repeat, consider adding
Round 6, knit in A.

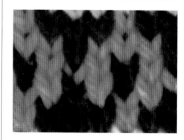

Hearts (worked in a multiple of 8 sts)

Round 1: With A, knit.
Round 2: *With A, k3, with B, k1, with A, k4; rep from * to end.
Round 3: *With A, k2, with B, k3, with A, k3; rep from * to end.
Round 4: *With A, k1, with B, k5, with A, k2; rep from * to end.
Rounds 5-6: *With B, k7, with A, k1; rep from * to end.
Round 7: *[With A, k1, with B, k2] twice, with A, k2;
rep from * to end.
Rounds 8–10: With A, knit.
Round 11: *With A, k7, with B, k1; rep from * to end.
Round 12: *With B, k1, with A, k5, with B, k2; rep from * to end.
Round 13: *With B, k2, with A, k3, with B, k3; rep from * to end.
Rounds 14-15: *With B, k3, with A, k1, with B, k4; rep from *
to end.
Round 16: *With B, k2, with A, k3, with B, k2, with A, k1; rep
from * to end.
Round 17-18: With A, knit.

Stitch Dictionary Part 2:

Cable and Texture Options

Using color is not the only way to add variety to your knits! Using textured stitch patterns or incorporating cables has an entirely different, but equally enticing, effect on the finished garment. Texture simply refers to using both knits and purls in some combination on the right side of the work. Perhaps the most widely used texture is ribbing. Cables are created by intentionally twisting stitches in a consistent pattern. The effect of the twisting differs depending on whether stitches are twisted behind or in front of each other, and whether there is movement across a specified area of the knitting. Cabling is used in a couple of ways in this book. Primarily, cables are used as a border or hem in many of the pieces. A few knits, however, feature cables as the main element of the design.

Cables and Gauge

The act of twisting stitches will always tighten up a knitter's gauge to some extent. This tightening makes cabled borders appealing for hats, mittens, and legwarmers particularly, as the extra snugness helps to hold the item in place. If you intend to use a cable as a main feature of the design, make sure to use the cable repeat in your gauge swatch. You might find that you need to go up several needle sizes and perhaps even use a heavier weight yarn in order to get the same gauge as a piece suggests for a stockinette or colorwork stitch pattern.

Texture and Gauge

Using knits and purls together can have the opposite effect on your gauge as cabling. Instead of tightening it, knitters often find that they loosen their tension as their yarn is moved from back to front, or front to back. This is why many patterns instruct using a smaller needle for a ribbed cuff or border than is used for the main body of the design. If you intend to use a texture pattern as a main feature of the design, make sure to use this texture in your gauge swatch. You might need to drop down a needle size or two.

Stitch Repeats

Just like incorporating colorwork, stitch repeats must be minded when substituting both cabled and textured stitch patterns. You'll want the stitch count total to divide evenly into the pattern. For more details, see the Stitch Repeats section in the Stitch Dictionary Part 1.

The Patterns

Each pattern is written either in "Rounds" or "Rows" depending on whether the sample was worked in the round, or flat. Most patterns are written to be knit in the round, but you may knit them flat provided that you adjust for knits and purls on the right and wrong side of the work. Remember, however, that if you are adjusting an in-the-round pattern to be worked back and forth, you'll want to make sure all cabled rows are worked on the right side. The easiest way to do this is to make the total number of rows an even number—just add or subtract a plain row if necessary. In these patterns, cabled rows are marked with RS to make them easy to spot.

Symbol Key

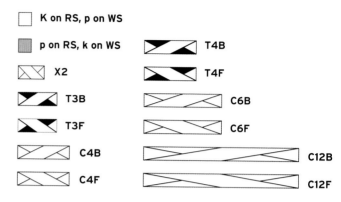

K on RS, p on WS	
p on RS, k on WS	T4B
X2	T4F
T3B	C6B
T3F	C6F
C4B	C12B
C4F	C12F

Crossover (worked over an even number of sts)

Rounds 1 & 2: Knit.
Round 3 (RS): *X2; rep from * to end.
Crossover is also used as a rib; any number of purled stitches can be added in between the two stitch repeat.

Crossover Rib (worked over a multiple of 4 sts)

Rounds 1 & 2: *K2, p2; rep from * to end.
Round 3 (RS): *X2, p2; rep from * to end.

Cabled Braid

This braid is featured in the Chunky Cabled Cap and Cabled Infinity Cowl. I've included a couple of smaller-multiple braids here if you'd like to incorporate them elsewhere.

Large Cabled Braid (worked over a multiple of 20 sts)

Round 1: *Knit 18, p2; rep from * to end.
Round 2 (RS): *C12F, k6, p2; rep from * to end.
Rounds 3-5: *K18, p2; rep from * to end.
Round 6 (RS): *K6, C12B, p2; rep from * to end.
Rounds 7-8: *K18, p2; rep from * to end.

Adjust the cabled braid to be worked over a different multiple by changing the background (purled) sts.

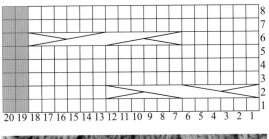

Medium Cabled Braid (worked over a multiple of 12 sts)

Round 1 (RS): *C6F, k3, p3; rep from * to end.
Rounds 2–4: *K9, p3; rep from * to end.
Round 5 (RS): *K3, C6B, p3; rep from * to end.
Rounds 6–8: *K9, p3; rep from * to end.

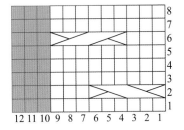

Small Cabled Braid (worked over a multiple of 8 sts)

Round 1: *K6, p2; rep from * to end.
Round 2 (RS): *C4F, k2, p2; rep from * to end.
Round 3: *K6, p2; rep from * to end.
Round 4 (RS): *K2, C4B, p2; rep from * to end.

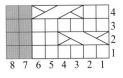

NORTHERN PLAINS
PUBLIC LIBRARY
Ault, Colorado

Cable Circles (worked over a multiple of 8 sts)

Round 1: *P2, k4, p2; rep from * to end.
Round 2 (RS): *P1, T3B, T3F, p1; rep from * to end.
Round 3: *P1, k2, p2, k2, p1 rep from * to end.
Round 4 (RS): *T3B, p2, T3F; rep from * to end.
Rounds 5–7: *k2, p4, k2; rep from * to end.
Round 8 (RS): *T3F, p2, T3B; rep from * to end.
Round 9: *P1, k2, p2, k2, p1; rep from * to end.
Round 10 (RS): *P1, T3F, T3B, p1; rep from * to end.

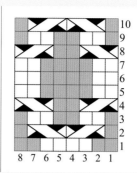

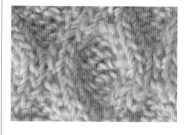

Crossing Cable Circles (worked over a multiple of 8 sts)

Round 1: *P2, k4, p2; rep from * to end.
Round 2 (RS): *P1, T3B, T3F, p1; rep from * to end.
Round 3: *P1, k2, p2, k2, p1 rep from * to end.
Round 4 (RS): *T3B, p2, T3F; rep from * to end.
Rounds 5–7: *K2, p4, k2; rep from * to end.
Round 8 (RS): *T3F, p2, T3B; rep from * to end.
Round 9: *P1, k2, p2, k2, p1; rep from * to end.
Round 10 (RS): *P1, T3F, T3B, p1; rep from * to end.
Round 11: *P2, k4, p2; rep from * to end.
Round 12 (RS): *P2, C4F, p2; rep from * to end.

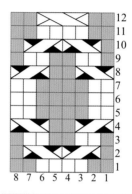

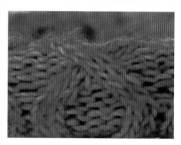

X Cable (worked over a multiple of 8 sts)

Round 1: *K2, p4, k2; rep from * to end.
Round 2 (RS): *T3F, p2, T3B; rep from * to end.
Round 3: *P1, k2, p2, k2, p1; rep from * to end.
Round 4 (RS): *P1, T3F, T3B, p1; rep from * to end.
Round 5: *P2, k4, p2; rep from * to end.
Round 6 (RS): *P2, C4F, p2; rep from * to end.
Round 7: *P2, k4, p2; rep from * to end.
Round 8 (RS): *P1, T3B, T3F, p1; rep from * to end.
Round 9: *P1, k2, p2, k2, p1; rep from * to end.
Round 10 (RS): *T3B, p2, T3F; rep from * to end.

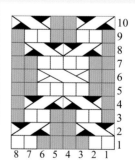

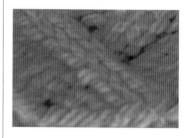

Cable Squiggles (worked over a multiple of 4 sts)

Row 1 (WS): *K2, p2; rep from * to end.
Row 2 (RS): *T4F; rep from * to end.
Rows 3–5: *P2, k2; rep from * to end.
Row 6 (RS): *T4B; rep from * to end.
Rows 8: *K2, p2; rep from * to end.

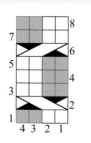

Cabled Rib (worked over a multiple of 8 sts)

Round 1: *K4, p4; rep from * to end.
Round 2 (RS): *C4F, p4; rep from * to end.
Round 3: *K4, p4; rep from * to end.
Adjust the cabled rib to be worked over a different multiple by changing the background (purled) stitches, as is exemplified in the Toddler & Teen sizes of the Elbow Mitts.

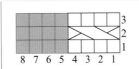

Moss Stitch (worked over an even number of sts)

Row 1: *K1, p1; rep from * to end.
Row 2 (RS): Knit.
Row 3: *P1, k1; rep from * to end.
Row 4: Knit.

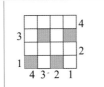

Ribbing

Ribbing describes a pattern in which an alternating repeat of knit and purl stitches are stacked on top of each other, row after row. Rib stitch patterns are included in many garments along hem or cuff lines to add shape and elasticity.

Garter Stitch

In a garter stitch pattern, knit rows and purl rows alternate on the right side of the work. When you are working back and forth, this simply means to knit every row. When working in the round, repeat the following two rounds:
Round 1 (RS): Knit.
Round 2: Purl.

Chapter 2

Heads

Chunky Cabled Cap

Loads of warmth is packed into this hat. Braided Cables create a thick, extra-long "brim," set off by a contrasting-color crown. Experiment by working this in a solid color, or by substituting a different cable pattern, such as Cable Squiggles or even a Crossover Rib. Shown here in child/teen.

Size
toddler (child/teen)

Finished Circumference
16½ (19¼)"
[42 (49) cm]

Gauge
15 sts and 19 rows per 4" (10 cm) in stockinette

18 st cable panel measures 2¾"(7 cm)

Yarn
- Berroco Vintage Chunky [50% acrylic, 40% wool, 10% nylon; 130 yds/120 m per 3.5 oz/100 g skein] 1 skein each Wasabi (A) and Bilberry (B) or 75 (115) yds [68.5 (105) m] A and 25 (35) yds [23 (32) m] B

Tools
- size 10 (6 mm) 16" (40.5 cm) circular needle
- set of 5 size 10 (6 mm) DPNs
- J (6mm) crochet hook
- stitch marker

LARGE CABLED BRAID

Large Cabled Braid

(worked over a multiple of 20 sts)

Round 1: *K18, p2; rep from * around.

Round 2: *C12F, k6, p2; rep from * around.

Rounds 3–5: *K18, p2; rep from * around.

Round 6: *K6, C12B, p2; rep from * around.

Rounds 7–8: *K18, p2; rep from * around.

Begin

With A and circular needles, CO 100 (120) sts.

Set-up Round: *K18, p2; rep from * around.

Next Round: *Work Large Cabled Braid over 20 sts; rep from * around.

Continue as established until hat measures 4 (5) inches [10 (12.5) cm] from CO edge, ending after Round 4 or 8.

Cut yarn and switch to B.

Next Round: *K2tog; rep from * to last 8 (0) sts, k to end: 54 (60) sts.

Knit in the round until hat measures 5½ (7)" [14 (18) cm] from CO edge.

Crown Shaping

Note: Switch to DPNs when necessary.

Round 1: *K4, k2tog;
rep from * around—45 (50) sts.

Round 2: Knit all sts.

Round 3: *K3, k2tog;
rep from * around—36 (40) sts.

Round 4: Knit all sts.

Round 5: *K2, k2tog;
rep from * around—27 (30) sts.

Round 6: Knit all sts.

Round 7: *K1, k2tog;
rep from * around—18 (20) sts.

Round 8: *K2tog;
rep from * around—9 (10) sts.

Finishing

Cut yarn, weave through remaining live sts and secure. Work one single crochet (page 17) in every stitch around CO edge of hat. Weave in all loose ends.

Zany
Stripes Hat

Neon colors are all the rage. And why shouldn't they be? They don't get any brighter than this fun cap, which is worked from the top down in the round and features stripes going every which way. Tone it down by working in only 2 colors or sticking with just one braided tassel. In addition to the Diagonal Stripes motif featured in the example, this pattern is well-suited for use with the Zigzag, Stripe & Dot, and many other stitch pattern options. Shown here in child/teen size.

Size
toddler (child/teen)

Finished Circumference
16 (18¾)"
[40.5 (47.5) cm]

Gauge
18 sts and 25 rows per 4" stitch (10 cm) in stockinette stitch

Yarn
- Madelinetosh Tosh Vintage [100% superwash merino wool; 200 yds/183 m per 3.9 oz/110 g skein] 1 skein each Citrus (A), Edison Bulb (B), Electric Chartreuse (C), and Robin's Egg (D) or 80 (90) yds [73 (82) m] C and 45 (55) yds [41 (50) m] each A, B, and D

Tools
- size 7 (4.5 mm) 16" (40.5 cm) circular needle
- set of 5 size 7 (4.5 mm) DPNs
- crochet hook

2-Row Even Stripes

Rounds 1–2: With B, knit.

Rounds 3–4: With A, knit.

2-ROW EVEN STRIPES

Going Left

(worked over a multiple of 4 sts)

Round 1: *With C, k2, with D, k2; rep from * around.

Round 2: *With D, k1, with C, k2, with D, k1; rep from * around.

GOING LEFT

Round 3: *With D, k2, with C, k2; rep from * around.

Round 4: *With C, k1, with D, k2, with C, k1; rep from * around.

Going Right

(worked over a multiple of 4 sts)

Round 1: *With C, k2, with D, k2; rep from * around.

Round 2: *With C, k1, with D, k2, with C, k1; rep from * around.

GOING RIGHT

Round 3: *With D, k2, with C, k2; rep from * around.

Round 4: *With D, k1, with C, k2, with D, k1; rep from * around.

Begin

With A, CO 6 sts. Divide these sts evenly among 3 DPNs. PM and join to work in the round, being careful not to twist sts. Knit 1 round.

Crown Shaping

Round 1: *K1, m1; rep from * around—12 sts.

Round 2: *K1, m1; rep from * around—24 sts.

Round 3: Knit.

Round 4: *K2, m1; rep from * around—36 sts.

Switch to B.

Round 5: *K3, m1; rep from * around—48 sts.

Round 6: Knit.

Switch to A.

Round 7: *K4, m1; rep from * around—60 sts.

Round 8: Knit.

Switch to B.

Round 9: *K5, m1; rep from * around—72 sts.

Round 10: *K6, m0 (1); rep from * around. 72 (84) sts.

Work 8 (10) rounds in Going Left.

Work 6 (10) rounds in 2-Row Even Stripes.

Work 8 (10) rounds in Going Right.

Beginning with Round 3, work 5 (9) rounds in 2-Row Even Stripes.

Next Round: BO 7 (10) sts. With spare DPN, k16 (19) sts and leave on holder for first ear flap, BO 24 (27) sts, k16 (19) sts for second ear flap, BO 6 (9) sts. Break yarn.

Ear Flaps

With D, work back and forth over 16 (19) sts in St st for 2" (5 cm), ending after a WS row.

Decrease Round: K1, ssk, work to last 3 sts, k2tog, k1—2 sts decreased.

Work Decrease Round every RS row a total of 4 (5) times. 8 (9) sts remain.

BO all sts. Repeat for remaining ear flap.

Finishing

With C, make a 2" (5 cm) pom-pom with 100 wraps (see page 17). Secure pom-pom to top of hat. Weave in all loose ends. Block.

Braided Tassel

(make 3 for each ear flap)

Cut four 30 (36)" [76 (91.5) cm] lengths of each A, B and C—12 strands.

Use crochet hook to pull strands halfway through bottom of each earflap—24 strands. Divide strands into 3 groups of 8 strands each and braid until 2" (5 cm) are left. Tie a knot to secure.

Hair Frills

Dress up the most basic of hair pieces with these quick and easy slide-on accessories. Better yet—make frills to match some of the other pieces you're knitting from this book! Shown here with headband for Flower Frill and hair clip for both the Bow Frill and Pomtastic Frill.

Size
one size

Gauge
22 sts and rows per 4" (10 cm) in stockinette

Yarn
• HiKoo Simplicity by Skacel [55% merino, 28% acrylic, 17% nylon; 117 yds/107 m per 1.8 oz./50 g skein]

Flower Frill
• 1 skein each #029 (A), #033 (B), and #015 (C) or 70 yds (64 m) A, 25 yds (23 m) B and scraps C

Bow Frill
• 1 skein each #049 (D) and #038 (E) or 20 yds (18 m) D and scraps E

Pomtastic Frill
• 1 skein each #034 (F), #007 (G), and #013 (H) or 15 yds (14 m) F, and scraps G and H

Tools
• set of size 5 (3.75 mm) DPNs

Notions
• headband or hair-clip for each Frill

• hot glue for securing items if desired

Flower Frill

Outer Layer

With A, CO 6 sts. Divide these sts evenly among 3 DPNs. PM and join to work in the round, being careful not to twist stitches.

Knit 1 round.

Increase Round: *K1, m1; rep from * around.

Repeat last 2 rows a total of 4 times—96 sts.

Knit 4 rounds.

Increase Round: *Kf&b&f in one st; rep from * around—288 sts.

Knit 3 rounds.

BO all sts.

Middle Layer

With B, CO 6 sts. Divide these sts evenly among 3 DPNs. PM and join to work in the round, being careful not to twist stitches.

Knit 1 round.

Increase Round: *K1, m1; rep from * around.

Repeat last 2 rows a total of 3 times—48 sts.

Knit 2 rounds.

Increase Round: *Kf&b&f in one st; rep from * around—144 sts.

Knit 3 rounds.

BO all sts.

Center

With C, CO 6 sts. Divide these sts evenly among 3 DPNs. PM and join to work in the round, being careful not to twist stitches.
Knit 1 round.

Increase Round: *K1, m1; rep from * around—12 sts.

Knit 1 round. Cut yarn, weave through rem sts and secure. Use a tapestry needle to weave loose ends to cast-on side of ball and tie firmly to flatten.

Tube

With C, CO 4 sts to a DPN. Work I-cord for 5 rounds. BO all sts.

Finishing

Use long tails from Center to attach all three layers of flower. Then thread these tails to inside of Tube, weaving in and out several times for sturdiness, making sure to leave tube open. Tie off tails inside tube. Weave in all loose ends. Slide tube onto hairband or hairclip. If needed, secure with more yarn and tapestry needle or hot glue.

BITTY DOTS

(chart grid with row numbers 6, 5, 4, 3, 2, 1 on right side and column numbers 4 3 2 1 at bottom)

Bitty Dots

(worked over a multiple of 4 sts)

Round 1: *With D, k1, with E, k1, with D, k2; rep from * around.

Rounds 2–3: With D, knit.

Round 4: *With D, k3, with E, k1; rep from * around.

Round 5–6: With D, knit.

Bow Frill

With D and a single DPN, CO 20 sts. With 2 DPNs, *sl 1 st to first DPN and next st to second DPN; repeat from * until all sts are divided evenly onto two DPNs. PM and join to work in the round. Knit 1 round.

Next Round: K10, pm, k to end.

Increase Round: *K1, m1R, k to one st before marker, m1L, k1; rep from * once more—24 sts.

Work even in Bitty Dots until piece measures 3 inches from CO edge.

Cut yarn for E.

Decrease Round: With D, *k2tog, k to 2 sts before marker, ssk; rep from * once more—20 sts.

Knit 3 rounds.

Flip piece inside out and weave in tails from B into the inside of the tie. Flip piece right side out.

Arrange sts so that the first 10 sts are on one DPN, and the second 10 are on another. Graft using Kitchener Stitch.

Knot

With D, CO 7 sts.

Sl first st of every row, and work back and forth in St st in until piece measures 2 inches from CO edge. BO all sts. Cut yarn, leaving long tail for sewing.

Squeeze the middle of the bowtie and tightly wrap knot strip around it. Seam knot ends together.

Slide onto hairband or hairclip. If needed, secure with more yarn and tapestry needle or hot glue.

Pomtastic Frill

Tube

With F, CO 4 sts. Work I-cord for 5 rounds. BO all sts.
Weave in all loose ends.

Pom-Poms (See page 17)

With F, make a 2"(5 cm) pom-pom with 50 wraps.

With G, make a 1"(2.5 cm) pom-pom with 30
wraps.

With H, make a 1"(2.5 cm) pom-pom with 30
wraps.

Use tapestry needle to thread tails from each
pom-pom into the tube and secure inside by
tying a knot.

Slide onto hairband or hairclip. If needed, secure
with more yarn and tapestry needle or hot glue.

Stripey Headband

This Boho-inspired headpiece is completely adjustable and whips up quickly. It's worked back and forth and has a crocheted edging and braided tassels to secure it. Make one, two, three, or more headbands in different color and stitch-pattern combinations. She can wear it with her favorite pair of flared pants ... or, better yet, you can make a headband to match a pair of leggings from the book!

Size
one size

Band Width
2" (5 cm)

Band Length
11" (28 cm)

Gauge
20 sts and 28 rows per 4" (10 cm) in stockinette stitch

Yarn
- Anzula For Better or Worsted [80% superwash merino, 10% cashmere, 10% nylon; 200 yds/183 m per 4.1 oz/115 g skein] 1 skein each Paradise (A) and Key Lime (B) or 30 yds (27 m) each A and B worsted weight yarn

Tools
- size 7 (4.5 mm) needles
- size H (5 mm) crochet hook

Choppy Stripes

Row 1 (RS): With A, *k2tog twice, kf&b twice; rep from * to end.

Row 2: With A, purl.

Row 3: With B, *k2tog twice, kf&b twice; rep from * to end.

Row 4: With B, purl.

CHOPPY STRIPES

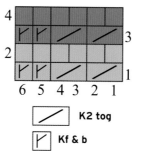

K2 tog

Kf & b

Begin

With A, CO 8 sts.

Purl 1 row. Do not cut yarn.

Switch to B.

Increase Row: K1, m1L, k to last st, m1R, k1—2 sts increased.

Purl 1 row. Do not cut yarn.

Switch to A. Work last 2 rows a total of 3 times, switching colors every 2 rows—14 sts.

Next row (RS): K1, work in Choppy Stripes pattern to last st, k1.

Work in Choppy Stripes as established until band measures 10" (25 cm) from CO edge, ending after a WS row. Discontinue Choppy Stripes, but continue switching colors every 2 rows during decreases.

Decrease Row: K1, ssk, knit to last 3 sts, k2tog, k1—2 sts decreased.

Purl 1 row.

Work last 2 rows a total of 3 times—8 sts.

BO all sts.

Finishing

With A, work single crochet (see page 17) around entire band.

Braided Tassels

(make 3 at each end)

With B, cut 18 strands that measure 36" (91 cm). Use crochet hook to pull 3 strands at a time between single crocheted border and edge of headband—6 strands. Hold two strands together and braid to last 2 inches (5 cm). Tie a knot and trim ends.

Weave in all loose ends. Block.

Wavy Stripes Slouch

Featuring funky, wavy stripes, a circular, cabled brim, and a ruched crown, this slouchy hat is sophisticated enough for your teenage daughter. In fact, this slouch will be so popular, you'll find yourself knitting more than one. The second time around, add a third color, change out the cable pattern in the brim, or even try an alternate stitch pattern in the body of the hat. The 12-stitch multiple makes both sizes suitable for almost all of the colorwork stitch pattern options in the dictionary. Shown here in teen size.

Size
child (teen)

Finished Circumference
16 (18½)"
[41 (47) cm]

Gauge
24 sts and 30 rows per 4" (10 cm) in Wavy Stripes on larger needles

Yarn
• Anzula Mariposa [75% alpaca, 25% silk; 135 yds/123 m per 2 oz/57 g skein] 1 skein each Hyacinth (A), Arizona (B) or 75 (100) yds [68.5 (91) m] each A and B

Tools
• size 4 (3.5 mm) 16" circular needles

• size 6 (4.0 mm) 16" circular needles and set of 5 DPNs

CABLE CIRCLES

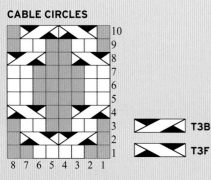

								10
								9
								8
								7
								6
								5
								4
								3
								2
								1

8 7 6 5 4 3 2 1

T3B

T3F

WAVY STRIPES

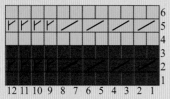

6
5
4
3
2
1

12 11 10 9 8 7 6 5 4 3 2 1

 KF&b

K2tog

Cable Circles

(worked over a multiple of 8 sts)

Round 1: *P2, k4, p2; rep from * around.

Round 2: *P1, T3B, T3F, p1; rep from * around.

Round 3: *P1, k2, p2, k2, p1; rep from * around.

Round 4: *T3B, p2, T3F; rep from * around.

Rounds 5–7: *k2, p4, k2; rep from * around.

Round 8: *T3F, p2, T3B; rep from * around.

Round 9: *P1, k2, p2, k2, p1; rep from * around.

Round 10: *P1, T3F, T3B, p1; rep from * around.

Wavy Stripes

(worked over a multiple of 12 sts)

Round 1: With B, knit.

Round 2: *K2tog 4 times, kf&b 4 times; rep from * around.

Round 3: Knit.

Rounds 4–6: With A, repeat Rounds 1–3.

Brim

With A and smaller needles, CO 104 (120) sts. PM and join to work in the round.

Work Rounds 1–10 of Cable Circles chart, then work Round 1 once more.

Hat

Switch to larger needles. Increase 4 (0) sts evenly during first round—108(120) sts.

Work in Wavy Stripes pattern until hat measures 6½ (8)" [16.5 (20) cm] from CO edge of brim, ending after round 3 or 6 of pattern.

Crown Shaping

Note: Continue color changes every three rounds throughout crown shaping.

Round 1: *K4, k2tog; rep from * around—90 (100) sts.

Round 2: *K3, k2tog; rep from * around—72(80) sts.

Round 3: *K2, k2tog; rep from * around—54(60) sts.

Round 4: *K1, k2tog; rep from * around—36(40) sts.

Round 5: *K2tog; rep from * around—18(20) sts.

Round 6: *K2tog; rep from * around—9(10) sts.

Finishing

Cut yarn, weave through rem sts and secure. Weave in all loose ends. Block.

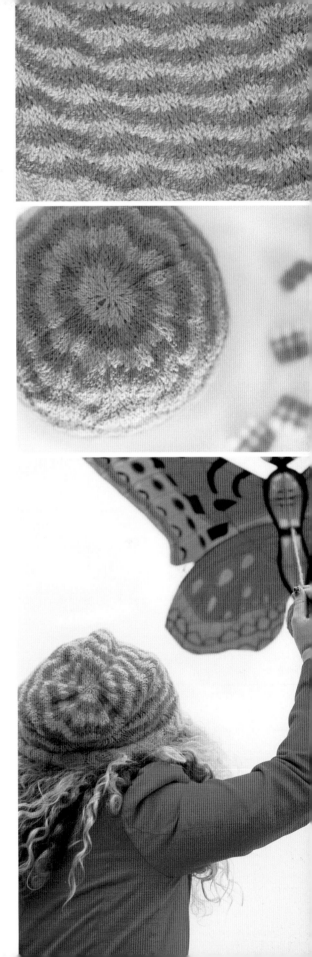

Harf

This chunky hat doubles as a warm and toasty scarf. Because of the gauge, the finished fabric is super stretchy, making it suitable for a large age range. Take no time troubling yourself about sizing! Try striping the scarf tail or including more stitch patterns in the hat itself.

Size
one size fits toddler through teen

Finished Hat Circumference
16" (40.5 cm)

Scarf Tail Length
36" (91 cm)

Gauge
15 sts and 18 rows per 4" (10 cm) in stockinette stitch

Yarn
- Malabrigo Yarn Chunky [100% merino; 104 yds/95 m per 3.5 oz/100 g skein] 3 skeins Apple Green (A) and 1 skein each Glazed Carrot (B) and Purple Mystery (C) or 220 yds (201 m) A and 55 yds (50.5 m) each B and C

Tools
- size 11(8 mm) 16" (40.5 cm) circular needles
- set of size 11 (8mm) DPNs

X Cable

(worked over a multiple of 8 sts)

Round 1: *K2, p4, k2; rep from * around.

Round 2: *T3F, p2, T3B; rep from * around.

Round 3: *P1, k2, p2, k2, p1; rep from * around.

Round 4: *P1, T3F, T3B, p1; rep from * around.

Round 5: *P2, k4, p2; rep from * around.

Round 6: *P2, C4F, p2; rep from * around.

Round 7: *P2, k4, p2; rep from * around.

Round 8: *P1, T3B, T3F, p1; rep from * around.

Round 9: *P1, k2, p2, k2, p1; rep from * around.

Round 10: *T3B, p2, T3F; rep from * around.

Medium Zigzag

(worked over a multiple of 4 sts)

Round 1: *With A, K3, with C, K1; rep from * around.

Round 2: *With C, k1, with A, k1, with C, k2; rep from * around.

Round 3: *With C, k3, with A, k1; rep from * around.

Round 4: *With A, k1, with C, k1, with A, k2; rep from * around.

MEDIUM ZIG ZAG

X CABLE

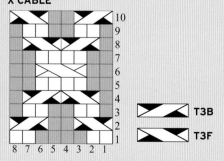

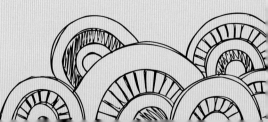

Hat

With B and circular needles, CO 64 sts. PM and join to work in the round, being careful not to twist stitches. Work Rounds 1–10 of X Cable once. Break yarn.

With A, knit 2 rounds.

*Work Rounds 1–4 of Medium Zigzag once. Break C.

With A, knit 2 rounds.

With B, knit 2 rounds. Break B.

With A, knit 2 rounds.

Repeat from * once more.

Crown Shaping

Note: Switch to DPNs when necessary.

Round 1: *K6, k2tog; rep from * around—56 sts.

Round 2: *K5, k2tog; rep from * around—48 sts.

Round 3: Knit.

Round 4: *K4, k2tog; rep from * around—40 sts.

Round 5: *K3, k2tog; rep from * around—32 sts.

Scarf Tail

Work even until scarf tail measures 36" (91 cm) from last round of crown shaping.

Next Round: *K2, k2tog; rep from * around—24 sts.

Knit 1 round.

Next Round: *K1, k2tog; rep from * around—16 sts.

Knit 1 round.

Next Round: *K2tog; rep from * around—8 sts.

Next Round: *K2tog; rep from * around—4 sts.

Cut yarn, weave through rem sts, and secure.

Pom-poms (see page 17)

Make a 3-inch (7.5 cm) pom-pom with 100 wraps with C for end of scarf.

Make 7 1-inch (2.5 cm) pom-poms with 20 wraps with B and 6 with C. Secure pom-poms randomly on all sides of scarf tail.

Finishing

Weave in all loose ends. Block.

Chapter 3

Shoulders

Mini Backpack

This backpack is perfect for holding all their treasures. It's worked from the bottom up, mostly in the round, and features just a smidge of intarsia during a short-row section in either a unisex or girly option. If intarsia isn't your thing, consider striping the pack (easier yet, use a self-striping yarn!) The pack is finished with I-cord edging, a drawstring, and a toggle to keep things safely inside. Shown here with the Flower Chart.

Size
one size

Gauge
20 sts and 28 rows per 4" (10 cm) in stockinette stitch

Yarn
- Lorna's Laces Shepherd Worsted [100% wool; 225 yds/206 m per 4 oz/114 g skein]; 1 skein each Tomfoolery (A), Lilac (B), Grant Park (C), and Catalpa (D) or 165 yds (151 m) A, 65 yds (59 m) B, 15 yds (14 m) C, and scraps of D

Tools
- size 7 (4.5 mm) 16" (40.6 cm) circular needles
- size 5 (3.75 mm) DPNs
- size H (5 mm) crochet hook
- sewing needle
- matching thread

Notions
- 2" (5 cm) toggle button

Base

With A and larger needles, provisionally CO 36 sts. Work back and forth in St st for 3" (7.5 cm).

Place provisionally CO sts on spare needle, ready to work RS.

Sides

Knit 18 sts on working needles, pm for end of round, k18, pick up and knit 15 sts along side, pm, knit across 36 sts from provisionally CO edge, pm, pick up and knit 15 sts along side. Join to work in the round—102 sts.

Work in the round for 1" (2.5).

Work short rows (see W&T, page 17) as follows:

Short Rows 1–2: Knit to second marker, W&T, purl to marker, W&T.

Short Rows 3–4: Knit to first marker, k8, pm, work Flower or Plane intarsia chart over 23 sts, pm, knit to next marker, knit to wrapped st, pick up wrap and work together with next st, W&T, work as established back to first marker, pick up wrap & work together with next st, W&T.

Repeat Short Rows 3–4 a total of 14 times, working intarsia chart once and removing markers when finished.

Resume working in the round once short rows are complete.

Next Round: K18, pm, k66, pm, k18.

Decrease Round: Knit to marker, sm, k2tog, k to 2 sts before marker, ssk, sm, k to end of round—2 sts decreased.

Work Decrease Round every other round a total of 12 times—78 sts.

Work even for 4 rounds.

Eyelet Round: *K4, yo, k2tog; rep from * around.

Work even for 4 rounds.

Next Rnd: Removing markers as you go, knit to second marker, sl previous 42 sts to holder—36 sts.

Front Flap

Knit 4 rows.

Decrease Row (RS): K1, ssk, k to last 3 sts, k2tog, k1—2 sts decreased.

Work Decrease Row every RS row a total of 10 times—16 sts.

Flap Edging

Place 42 sts from top of bag on spare needle, ready to work RS. Place 16 sts from front of flap on spare needle. With C and RS facing, pick up and knit 18 sts on right side of flap, k16 sts on front of flap, pick up and knit 18 sts on left side of flap, knit across 42 sts for top of bag—92 sts. Join as though to work in the round.

Using I-cord bind-off method (page 17), BO all sts.

Straps

Use 2 DPNs and B to work back and forth for each strap as follows:

Pick up and knit 5 sts at back top corner of bag. Work in I-cord (page 15) until strap measures 18" (46 cm). BO all sts. Seam bottom of strap to corresponding bottom corner.

Drawstring

Use 2 DPNs and C to work back and forth for drawstring as follows: CO 3 sts. Work in I-cord (page 15) until drawstring measures 20" (51 cm) from CO. BO all sts.

Buttonhole

Use 2 DPNs and C to work back and forth for "buttonhole" as follows: CO 3 sts. Work in I-cord until piece measures 3" (7.5 cm) from CO edge. BO all sts. Sew each end of I-cord, making a loop, to underside of front center panel.

Finishing

Weave in all loose ends. Block. Starting at front corner, weave drawstring in and out of eyelets. Tie a cute little bow. Using sewing needle and matching thread, sew button to front flap about halfway between top of intarsia chart and drawstring.

FLOWER INTARSIA CHART

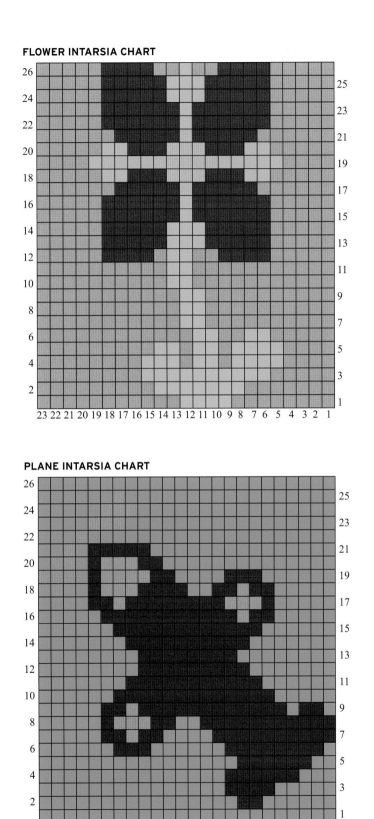

PLANE INTARSIA CHART

NORTHERN PLAINS
PUBLIC LIBRARY
Ault, Colorado

Reversible Scarf

This cozy scarf looks just as good on one side as the other because the blocks alternate between stockinette and reverse stockinette. Knit it in as many or few colors as you'd like. It will fit everyone in the house, so be sure to get extra yardage so you can make one for everyone.

Size
one size

Width
6" (15 cm)

Length
65" (165 cm)

Gauge
17 sts and 21 rows per 4" (10 cm) in stockinette stitch

Yarn
- Caron Vickie Howell Sheep(ish) [70% acrylic, 30% wool; 167 yds/153 m per 3 oz/85 g skein] 1 skein each Gun Metal(ish) (A), Turquoise(ish) (B), Red(ish) (C) and Chartreuse(ish) (D) or 85 yds (78 cm) A, 60 yds (55 cm) each B and D, and 110 yds (100.5 cm) C

Tools
- size 8 (5 mm) needles
- size H (5 mm) crochet hook

Pattern notes
The chart shows the color changes used in the sample. Refer to the chart for color and stitch changes.

Scarf

CO 25 sts. Purl 1 WS row.

Block 1

Work back and forth in St st until piece measures 5" (12.5 cm), ending after a WS row. Cut yarn. Switch to new color.

Block 2

Color Changing Row: *K1, p1; rep from * around.

Next row (WS): Knit.

Work back and forth in Rev St st (purl the RS rows and knit the WS rows) until second block measures 5" (12.5 cm), ending after a RS row. Cut yarn. Switch to new color.

Block 3

Work Color Changing Row from Block 2.

Next row (RS): Knit.

Work back and forth in St st until third block measures 5" (12.5 cm), ending after a WS row. Cut yarn. Switch to new color.

Work Blocks 2 and 3 a total of 6 times (13 blocks), using the chart as a guide for color and stitch pattern changes. BO all sts.

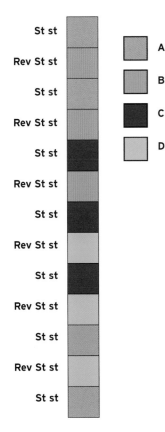

St st	
Rev St st	
St st	
Rev St st	
St st	
Rev St st	
St st	
Rev St st	
St st	
Rev St st	
St st	
Rev St st	
St st	

	A
	B
	C
	D

Finishing

Edging

With C and crochet hook, begin at one corner of the scarf and work single crochet (page 17) around entire edge of scarf. To make the scarf fully reversible and symmetrical on both sides, crochet into middle of the edge stitch instead of leaving a selvedge edge. Do not break yarn at corners.

Tassels

Cut 25 lengths of yarn, each measuring 8" (20 cm). Fold each strand in half and use crochet hook to draw the loop at the middle through one stitch on one short end of the scarf. Pull both ends of the strand through the loop snugly. Repeat for each strand, on each stitch. Trim tassels so that ends are even. Repeat process for other end of scarf.

Block.

Cabled Infinity Cowl

Wear it long or doubled, as a scarf, necklace, or cowl—there are lots of options here. Try alternate cable patterns like the X or Circular options. The project is worked in the round and then the cast-on and bind-off edges are seamed.

Size
one size

Width
4" (10 cm)

Circumference
48" (122 cm)

Gauge
10 sts and 19 rows per 4" (10 cm) in reverse stockinette stitch

18 stitch cable panel measures approximately 3½" (9 cm)

Yarn
- Lion Brand Alpine Wool [100% wool; 93 yds/85 m per 3 oz/85 g skein] 4 skeins Blueberry or 300 yds (274 m)

Tools
- size 11(8 mm) 40" (102 cm) circular needles

Large Cabled Braid

(worked over 18 sts)

Round 1: K18.

Round 2: C12F, k6.

Rounds 3–5: K18.

Round 6: K6, C12B.

Rounds 7–8: K18.

Cowl

CO 174 sts. PM and join to work in the round.

Set-up Round: *P5, k18, p6; rep from * around.

Next Round: *P5, work Large Cabled Braid over 18 sts, p6; rep from * around.

Continue as established until piece measures 8" (20 cm) from CO edge, ending after working Round 4 or 8 of Large Cabled Braid.

BO all sts.

Finishing

Seam CO edge and BO edge. Weave in all loose ends. Block.

LARGE CABLED BRAID

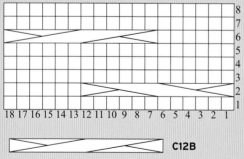

C12B

C12F

Ruffled Capelet

This project is sweet and dreamy with ruffles around the neck and cascading down the back. A simple bow secures it. For safety, the ribbon halves snap together in the back. Don't forget to knit the coordinating Ruffled Cufflets. Shown here in Child.

Size
toddler (child/teen)

Finished Circumference
23(27, 31½)" [58 (68.5, 80) cm]

Back Length
11 (12½, 14½)" [28 (32, 37) cm]

Gauge
26 sts and 34 rows per 4" (10 cm) in stockinette stitch

Yarn
• Shibui Knits Sock [100% merino; 191 yds/175 m per 1.8 oz/50 g skein] 3 (4, 5) skeins Kiwi or 475 (625, 810) yds [434 (571.5, 741) m]

Tools
• size 4 (3.5 mm) 40" 9102 cm) circular needles

Notions
• Marsha Neal Studios Handpainted Silky Ribbon in #99 Lime or 1 yd (1 m) ribbon

• sew-on snap

Pattern Notes
Circumference measured around shoulders.

CO 195 (231, 267) sts. Work back and forth in st st, slipping first st of every row, as follows:

Work even until piece measures 2" (5 cm) from CO edge, ending after a WS row.

Decrease Row: *K3tog; rep from * around—65 (77, 89) sts.

Work 3 rows.

Eyelet Row: Sl 1, k1 (2, 2), *[yo]twice, k2tog, k2, [yo]twice, k2tog, k5; rep from * to last 8 (8, 9) sts, [yo]twice, k2tog, k2, [yo]twice, k2tog, k to end.

Work 3 rows, dropping first yo of each eyelet on first row.

Increase Row 1: Sl 1, k2, m1, *k3, m1; rep from * to last 2 sts, k2—86 (102, 118) sts.

Work 3 rows.

Increase Row 2: Sl 1, k3, m1, *k4, m1; rep from * to last 2 sts, k2—107 (127, 147) sts.

Work 3 rows.

Increase Row 3: Sl 1, k4, m1, *k5, m1; rep from * to last 2 sts, k2—128 (152, 176) sts.

Work 3 rows.

Increase Row 4: Sl 1, k5, m1, *k6, m1; rep from * to last 2 sts, k2—149 (177, 205) sts.

Work even until capelet measures 3½ (5, 7)" [9 (12.5, 18) cm] from eyelet row, ending after a WS row.

Increase Row 5: Sl 1, *m1, k1; rep from * to end of row—297 (353, 409) sts.

Work even for 2" (5 cm).

BO first 3 sts of every row for the next 46 rows—159 (215, 271) sts.

BO all rem sts.

Finishing

Weave in all loose ends. Cut the ribbon in half. Fold under one end of each and sew on a snap. Thread ribbon in and out of eyelets, keeping ribbon on RS of capelet over longer segments and centering the snap at the back.

Colorblock Cowl

The blocks in this neckwarmer are worked in different textures and different colors. To change it up, mix and match stitch patterns as you like and consider using buttons at the neck instead of a zipper.

Size
one size

Width
6" (15 cm)

Length
19" (48 cm)

Gauge
12 sts and 15 rows per 4" (10 cm) in stockinette stitch

Yarn
- Spud & Chloë Outer [65% wool, 35% cotton; 60 yds/55 m per 3.5 oz/100 g skein] 1 skein each Wave (A), Cedar (B), Bayou(C), and Carbon(D) or 30 yds (27 m) each A, B, C, and D

Tools
- size 11(8 mm) needles
- sewing needle

Notions
- 7" (18 cm) separating zipper, shown with 2-way separating zipper
- matching thread

Pattern Notes
Width varies slightly between each panel, with the cabled panel being narrower and the textured panels wider than the stockinette panel.

Moss Stitch

(worked over an even number of sts)

Row 1: *K1, p1; rep from * to end.

Row 2 (RS): Knit.

Row 3: *P1, k1; rep from * to end.

Row 4: Knit.

MOSS STITCH

Cable Squiggles

(worked over a multiple of 4 sts)

Row 1 (WS): *K2, p2; rep from * to end.

Row 2 (RS): *T4F; rep from * to end.

Rows 3–5: *P2, k2; rep from * to end.

Row 6: *T4B; rep from * to end.

Rows 7–8: *K2, p2; rep from * to end.

CABLE SQUIGGLES

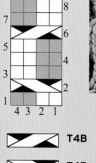

 T4B

T4F

Cowl Panel 1

With A, work zipper casing.

Zipper Casing

*CO 20 sts.

Row 1 (WS): Purl.

Row 2 (RS): Knit.

Cut yarn and slip sts to spare needles.

Repeat from * once more to make a second Zipper Casing.

Join zipper casing as follows: Holding pieces together with WS facing, *use working needle and yarn to knit the first stitch from front needle together with the first stitch from back needle. Repeat from * to end of row—20 sts.

Establish Moss Stitch as follows:

Row 1 (WS): Sl 1, work Moss St to last st, p1.

Row 2 (RS): Sl 1, work Moss St to last st, k1.

Continue Moss Stitch as established until panel measures 5" (12.5 cm) from CO edge, ending after a WS row. Cut yarn and switch to B.

Cowl Panel 2

Next Row (RS): Sl 1, knit to end of row.

Establish Cable Squiggles as follows:

Row 1 (WS): Sl 1, k1, work Cable Squiggles until 2 sts remain, k1, p1.

Row 2 (RS): Sl 1, p1, work Cable Squiggles until 2 sts remain, p2.

Continue Cable Squiggles as established until second panel measures 4½" (11 cm), ending after a WS row. Cut yarn. Slip stitches to spare needle and set aside.

Cowl Panel 3

With C, work Zipper Casing.

Knit every row for garter stitch, slipping first stitch on every row until panel measures 5" (12.5 cm) from CO edge. Cut yarn and switch to D.

Cowl Panel 4

Work in St st, slipping first stitch on every row until final panel measures 4½" (11 cm) from CO edge. Cut yarn leaving a tail 4 times the length of the stitches on working needles.

Finishing

Join Panel Sections

Using the long tail from panel 4, graft panel 2 and panel 4 together with Kitchener stitch (page 16).

Sew zipper inside casing. Weave in all loose ends.

Chapter 4

Knees

Button-Up Slouch Warmers

These sassy legwarmers have a built in slouch. Wear them with buttons at the side or the back, or even with a button or two undone. Have fun picking out the buttons—they really add personality to this pair! Shown here in child size.

Size
toddler(child, teen)

Calf Circumference
7½ (9, 10½)" [19 (23, 26.5) cm]

Length
7½ (9½, 14½)" [19 (24, 37) cm]

Gauge
15 sts and 24 rows per 4" (10 cm) in Waffle Rib on smaller needles

Yarn
- Blue Sky Alpacas Techno [68% baby alpaca, 22% silk, 10% extra fine merino; 120 yds/109 m per 1.8 oz/50 g skein] 1(2, 2) skeins Lounge Purple (A) and 1 skein Atomic Green (B) or 55 (130, 220) yds [50 (119, 201) m] A and 65 (80, 105) yds [59 (73, 96) m] B

Tools
- size 8(5 mm) needles
- size 9(5.5 mm) needles

Notions
- Heyday Handmade large fabric buttons 6 (8, 10)

Pattern Notes
Length is measured along button band and accounts for slouch.

Waffle Rib

(worked flat over a multiple of 3 sts)

Row 1 (WS): P1, k1, *p2, k1; rep from * to last st, p1.

Row 2 (RS): K1, *p1, k2; rep from * to last 2 sts, p1, k1.

Row 3: P1, knit to last st, p1.

Row 4: Work as for Row 2.

Leg (Make 2)

With B and smaller needles, CO 24 (30, 36) sts.

Work Rows 1–4 of Waffle Rib 3 times, then work Row 1 once more.

Cut yarn. Switch to A and larger needles.

Increase Row (RS): *K3, m1; rep from * to last 3 sts, k3—31 (39, 47) sts.

Work 7 rows in St st.

Decrease Row (RS): K1, ssk, k to last 3 sts, k2tog, k1—2 sts decreased.

Work Decrease Row every 6 (8, 12) rows a total of 4 (6, 8) times—23 (27, 31) sts.

Work even in St st until piece measures 8 (12, 17)" [20 (30.5, 43) cm] from CO edge, ending after a WS row.

Cut yarn. Switch to B and smaller needles.

Decrease Row (RS): *K2, k2tog; rep from * to last 3 sts, k3—18 (21, 24)sts.

Work Rows 1–4 of Waffle Rib 3 times, then work Row 1 once more. BO all sts.

Buttonband

Note: Work buttonholes on right side of one warmer, and left side of second warmer.

With B, pick up and knit 7 sts in waffle section, 11 (19, 37) sts in St st section, and 7 sts in waffle section—25 (33, 51) sts. Note: Number of sts picked up in St st section is less than normal in order to create slouch effect.

Next Row (WS): *P1, k1; rep from * to last st, p1.

Work in 1x1 rib as set for a total of 5 rows. BO all sts.

Pick up sts in same manner on other side of warmer. Work 2 rows in 1x1 rib.

Next Row (WS): K4, *work 3-st one-row buttonhole (see page 17), k3 (3, 5); rep from * a total of 3 (4, 5) times, knit to end.

Work 2 more rows in 1x1 rib. BO all sts.

Finishing

Sew 3 (4, 5) buttons opposite buttonholes on each warmer. Weave in all loose ends. Block.

Leggings

These form-fitting leggings are full of color to brighten up a grey, winter day. If stranded colorwork isn't your thing, just think how cute they would be in stripes. Consider using a lighter weight yarn at gauge for spring- or fall-weather wear. The leggings are fully shaped through the hip and can be knit in full or capri length. Shown here in size 8.

Size
5 (8, 11, 14) years

Waist
20¾ (21¾, 23½, 25½)" [52.5 (55, 60, 65) cm]

Gauge
17 sts and 21 rows per 4" (10 cm) in stockinette stitch

Yarn
- Spud & Chloë Sweater [55% wool, 45% cotton; 160 yds/146 m per 3.5 oz/100 g skein]

For Capri-length Leggings
2 (2, 2, 3) skeins Popsicle (A), 1 skein each Splash (B) and Penguin (C) or 190 (270, 315, 370) yds [174 (247, 288, 338) m] A, 50 (90, 120, 140) yds [46 (82, 110, 128) m] each B and C

For Full-length Leggings
2 (2, 3, 3) skeins Popsicle (A), 1 (1, 1, 2) skeins each Splash (B) and Penguin (C) or 205 (285, 330, 385) yds [187 (260.5, 302, 352) m] A, 70 (115, 140, 170) yds [64 (105, 128, 155) m] each B and C

Tools
- size 6 (4 mm) and size 7 (4.5 mm) 16" (40.6 cm) circular needles
- size 6 (4mm) and size 7 (4.5 mm) DPNs
- sewing needle

Notions
- waist circumference length of 1" (2.5 cm) wide elastic
- thread

Pattern Notes: Leggings are stretchy and sized with negative ease; waist measurement should be smaller than recipient.

Stripe & Dot

(worked over an even number of sts)

Round 1: With A, knit.

Round 2: With B, knit.

Round 3: *With B, k1, with C, k1; rep from * around.

Round 4: With B, knit.

Round 5: With A, knit.

Round 6: With C, knit.

Round 7: *With C, k1, with B, k1; rep from * around.

Round 8: With C, knit.

STRIPE & DOT

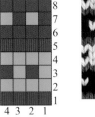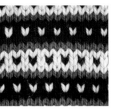

Waist

With smaller circular needles, CO 88 (92, 100, 108) sts.

Rib: *K1, p1; rep from * around. Place end of round marker; join in the round.

Work in Rib for 1½" (4 cm). Purl 1 round. Work Rib for 1½" (4 cm) more.

Fold work so that purled edge becomes top of cuff.

Joining Round (RS): Join working sts to cast-on edge as follows, * with left needle, pick up the first st from the cast-on edge and k2tog with next working st, repeat from * to last 4 sts, k4. (This leaves a hole for inserting elastic later.)

Hips

Switch to larger needles. Work short rows (W&T, page 17) as follows, picking up wraps on each row after they are placed:

Short Rows 1–2: K5, W&T, p9, W&T.

Short Rows 3–4: K13, W&T, p17, W&T.

Short Rows 5–6: K21, W&T, p25, W&T.

Short Rows 7–8: K29, W&T, p33, W&T.

Short Rows 9–10: K37, W&T, p41, W&T.

Sizes (8, 11, 14) ONLY: Short Rows 11–12: K45, W&T, p49, W&T.

Size 14 ONLY: Short Rows 13–14: K53, W&T, p57, W&T.

All sizes:

Knit to end of round marker.

Next Round: K22 (23, 25, 27), pm, k1, pm, k43 (45, 49, 53), pm, k1, pm, k to end.

Increase Round: *Knit to marker, sm, m1R, knit to marker, m1L, sm; repeat from * once more, k to end—4 sts increased.

Work Increase Round on next round and every 21 (5, 5, 5) rounds a total of 2 (6, 7, 8) times—96 (116, 128, 140) sts.

Place additional markers for crotch shaping as follows:

Next Round: *K1, pm, [work to next marker, sm] twice, k21 (22, 24, 26), pm; rep from * once more.

Crotch Shaping Round: *M1R, work to marker, m1L, sm, [work to next marker, sm] three times; repeat from * once more—4 sts increased.

Work one round even, then work Crotch Shaping Round once more.

Work Increase Round once more—108 (128, 140, 152) sts.

Sizes (8, 11, 14) ONLY: Work Crotch Shaping Round once more— (132, 144, 156) sts.

(continued)

All sizes:

Separate for Legs

Next round: Removing all markers as you go, k6 (8, 8, 8), sl previous 7 (9, 9, 9) sts to scrap yarn for back of crotch, work past next two markers to one stitch before next crotch section, sl previous 47 (57, 63, 69) sts to scrap yarn and place on hold for right leg, work 7 (9, 9, 9) sts, sl previous 7 (9, 9, 9) sts to scrap yarn for front of crotch, work to end. PM and join to work left leg in the round. 47 (57, 63, 69) sts each leg, 7 (9, 9, 9) sts for front and back of crotch.

Leg

Work even for 5 rounds.

Next Round: K1, k2tog, knit to end—46 (56, 62, 68) sts.

Begin Stripe & Dot pattern and work even for 5 rounds.

Decrease Round: K1, k2tog, work to last 3 sts, ssk, k1—2 sts decreased.

Full-length leggings: Repeat Decrease Round every 6 rounds a total of 12 (15, 17, 19) times—22 (26, 28, 30) sts. Work even in pat until leg measures 15 (20, 23, 25)" [38 (51, 58, 63.5) cm] from crotch, ending after Round 1 or 5 of Stripe & Dot pattern. Cut B and C.

Capri-length leggings: Work Decrease Round every 6 rounds a total of 8 (11, 13, 15) times—30 (34, 36, 38) sts. Work even in pat until leg measures 11 (16, 19, 21)" [28 (40.5, 48, 53) cm] from crotch, ending after Round 1 or 5 of Stripe & Dot pattern. Cut B and C.

Both versions:

Switch to smaller needles. With A, work Rib as for Waistband for 8 rounds. BO all sts with Jeny's Surprisingly Stretchy Bind-off (page 17).

Work right leg as for left.

Finishing

Graft front and back crotch sts together using Kitchener stitch. Insert elastic into waistband, sew ends of elastic together with needle and thread, and seam hole closed with tapestry needle. Weave in all loose ends. Block.

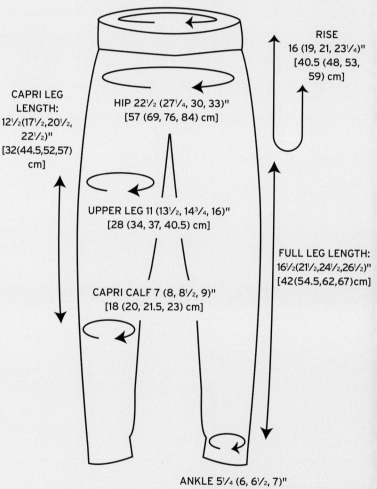

WAIST 20³/₄ (21³/₄, 23¹/₂, 25¹/₂)" [52.5 (55, 60, 65) cm]

RISE 16 (19, 21, 23¹/₄)" [40.5 (48, 53, 59) cm]

CAPRI LEG LENGTH: 12¹/₂ (17¹/₂, 20¹/₂, 22¹/₂)" [32 (44.5, 52, 57) cm]

HIP 22¹/₂ (27¹/₄, 30, 33)" [57 (69, 76, 84) cm]

UPPER LEG 11 (13¹/₂, 14³/₄, 16)" [28 (34, 37, 40.5) cm]

FULL LEG LENGTH: 16¹/₂ (21¹/₂, 24¹/₂, 26¹/₂)" [42 (54.5, 62, 67) cm]

CAPRI CALF 7 (8, 8¹/₂, 9)" [18 (20, 21.5, 23) cm]

ANKLE 5¹/₄ (6, 6¹/₂, 7)" [13 (15, 16.5, 18) cm]

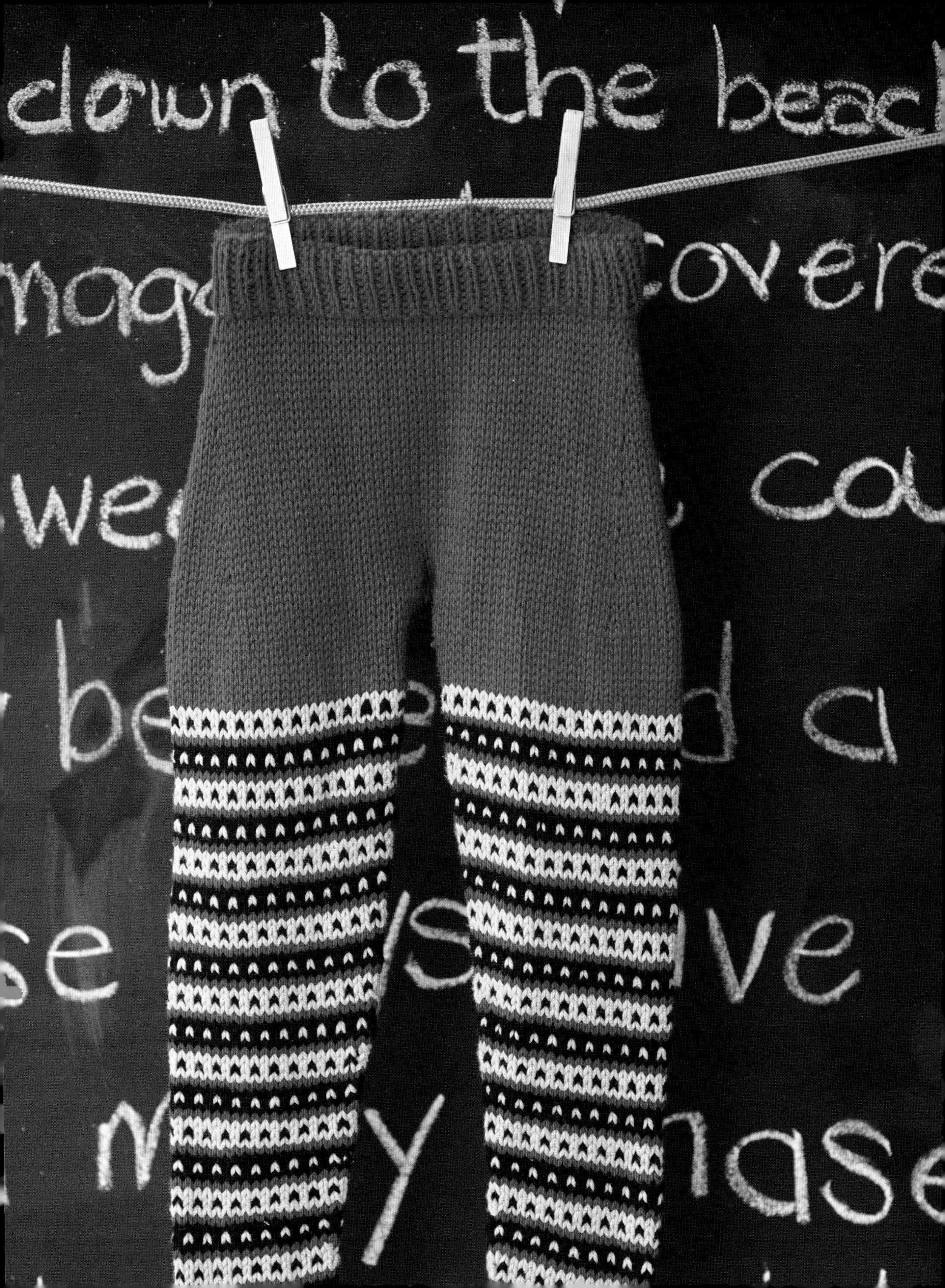
down to the

Legwarmers

Asymmetry makes these warmers pop. They are worked top down in the round and accentuated with a skinny cabled rib. Utility doesn't end at the calves, either—try these versatile warmers on the wrists, too. The Stripe & Dot and Vertical Stripe stitch patterns are great substitute colorwork options. Shown here in toddler size.

Size
toddler (child, tween)

Width (unstretched)
6½(7¼, 8)" [16.5(18, 20) cm]

Length
8¼(10, 12)" [21(25, 30) cm]

Gauge
20 sts and 25 rows per 4" (10 cm) in stockinette stitch

Yarn
• Ewe Ewe Wooly Worsted [100% merino wool; 95 yds/87 m per 1.8 oz/50 g skein] 1 skein each Berry (A), Pistachio (B), and Eggplant (C) or 70 (90, 120) yds [64 (82, 110) m] each A, B, and C

Tools
• set of size 7 (4.5 mm) DPNs

• stitch marker

Crossover Rib

(worked over a multiple of 4 sts)

Rounds 1–2: *K2, p2; rep from * around.

Round 3 (Crossover Round): *X2, p2; rep from * around.

CROSSOVER RIB

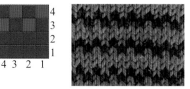

Little Zigzag

(worked over an even number of sts)

Rounds 1–2: With A, knit.

Round 3: *With A, k1, with C, k1; rep from * around.

Round 4: *With C, k1, with A, k1; rep from * around.

LITTLE ZIGZAG

Uneven Stripes

(worked over 8 rounds)

Rounds 1–2: Work in B.

Round 3: Work in C.

Rounds 4–5: Work in B.

Rounds 6–8: Work in C.

UNEVEN STRIPES

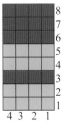

Striped Legwarmer

Calf Cuff

With A, CO 32 (36, 40) sts. Divide evenly among 3 DPNs. PM and join to work in the round.

Work the three rounds of Crossover Rib a total of 2 (3, 4) times. Work one more round in 2x2 rib. Cut yarn.

Leg

Work 1 round in Uneven Stripes pattern.

Decrease Round: Working next round in Uneven Stripe pattern as established, k1, k2tog, work to last three stitches, ssk, k1—2 sts decreased.

Continuing Uneven Stripes pattern as established, repeat Decrease Round on next round and every 10 (12, 14) rounds 3 more times—24 (28, 32) sts, ending after Round 2 or 5 of Uneven Stripes Pattern. Cut yarn.

Ankle Cuff

With A, knit 1 round. Work Rounds 2 and 3 of Crossover Rib, work Rounds 1–3 1 (2, 3) more times, then work Rounds 1 and 2 once more. BO all sts.

Zigzag Legwarmer

Calf Cuff

With B, work Calf Cuff as for Striped Legwarmer. Cut yarn.

Leg

Work 1 round in Little Zigzag pattern.

Decrease Round: Working next round in Little Zigzag pattern as established, k1, k2tog, work to last three stitches, ssk, k1—2 sts decreased.

Note: If Decrease Round is worked during either Round 3 or 4 of Little Zigzag pattern, make sure to adjust the following round so that contrasting colors are worked on alternating sts when compared to the previous round.

Continuing Little Zigzag pattern as established, repeat Decrease Round every 10 (12, 14) rounds 3 more times—24 (28, 32) sts, ending after Round 2 of Little Zigzag pattern. Cut yarn.

Ankle Cuff

With B, work Ankle Cuff as for Striped Legwarmer.

Finishing

Weave in all loose ends. Block.

Grounded Warmers

Jailer stripes with a twist, these legwarmers feature a spiraling black and white stitch pattern and a faux seam down the back. They are worked from the top down and finished with a ruffle. They are designed to come up over the knee, but smaller sizes can be worn shorter by older girls. Shown here in child size.

Size
toddler (child, teen)

Circumference (unstretched)
8¾ (10¾, 12½)" [22 (27, 31.5) cm]

Length
10¼ (14¾, 17¼)" [26 (37, 44) cm]

Gauge
18 sts and 22 rows per 4" (10 cm) in stockinette stitch

Yarn
- Lion Brand Yarn Wool-Ease [70% acrylic, 20% wool, 10% polyamide; 162 yds/146 m per 2.5 oz/70 g skein] 1 skein White Frost (A) or 65 (120, 165) yds [59 (110, 151) m]

- Lion Brand Yarn Wool-Ease [80% acrylic, 20% wool; 197 yds/180 m per 3 ounce/85 g skein] 1 skein each Black (B) and Ranch Red (C) or 55(110, 150) yds [50(100.5, 137) m] B and 30 (40, 45) yds [27 (36.5, 41) m] C

Tools
- size 6 (4 mm) DPNs
- size 7 (4.5 mm) DPNs
- sewing needle

Notions
- 8 (10, 11½)" [20 (25, 29) cm] length of 1" (2.5 cm) wide elastic; thread

Pattern Notes
Choose a size that is smaller than actual knee girth.

NORTHERN PLAINS
PUBLIC LIBRARY
Ault, Colorado

Spiral

(worked over a multiple of 8 sts)

Round 1: *With B, k4, with A, k4; rep from * around.

Round 2: *With B, k3, with A, k4, with B, k1; rep from * around.

Round 3: *With B, k2, with A, k4, with B, k2; rep from * around.

Round 4: *With B, k1, with A, k4, with B, k3; rep from * around.

Round 5: *With A, k4, with B, k4; rep from * around.

Round 6: *With A, k3, with B, k4, with A, k1; rep from * around.

Round 7: *With A, k2, with B, k4, with A, k2; rep from * around.

Round 8: *With A, k1, with B, k4, with A, k3; rep from * around.

Ribbed Top Cuff

With C and smaller DPNs, CO 40 (48, 56) sts. Divide sts evenly among 3 DPNs. PM and join to work in the round, being careful not to twist stitches.

Rib: *K2, p2; rep from * around.

Work in Rib for 1½" (4 cm). Purl 1 row. Resume Rib for 1½" (4 cm) inches.

Fold work so that purled edge becomes top of cuff.

Joining Round (RS): Join working sts to cast-on edge as follows, * with left needle, pick up the first st from the cast-on edge and k2tog with next working st, repeat from * to last 4 sts, k4. (This leaves a hole for inserting elastic later.)

Switch to larger needles.

SPIRAL

Leg

Establish Spiral pattern as follows:

Next Round: With C, k1, work Spiral pattern 4 (5, 6) times, work first 6 sts of Spiral pattern once more, with C (pull strand backwards gently), k1.

Work 4 (5, 6) rounds even.

Note: Adjust the Spiral pattern as necessary as sts are decreased so that center sts remain in pattern.

Decrease Round: With C, k1, maintaining Spiral pattern as established, ssk, work to last 3 sts, k2tog, with C, k1.

Repeat Decrease Round every 5 (6, 7) rounds a total of 8 (9, 10) times—24 (30, 36) sts.

Work even in pat until Leg measures 8¾ (13¼, 15¾)" [22 (33.5, 40) cm] from top of cuff. Cut yarn for A and C and work ruffled cuff solid in B.

Increase Round: *Kf&b&f in one st; rep from * around—72 (90, 108) sts.

Knit in the round until ruffle measures 1½" (4 cm) from increase round. BO all sts.

Finishing

Insert elastic in cuff, securing ends together with sewing needle and thread, and seam hole closed with tapestry needle. Weave in all loose ends. Block.

Lacy Legs

Accented with ribbons and ruffles, these warmers are worked flat and feature a corset effect up the back which also serves to size them perfectly for any wearer. Because the back of the leg is left open, they will fit toddler to teen. Any of the striping patterns from this book will work well. They are constructed top down and are shaped to form to the calf and ankle.

Size
One size that "grows"!

Width (unstretched)
8" (20 cm) knit with adjustable width behind laces

Length
14" (35.5 cm)

Gauge
18 sts and 22 rows per 4" (10 cm) in stockinette stitch

Yarn
• Caron Vickie Howell Sheep(ish) [70% acrylic, 30% wool; 167 yds/153 m per 3 oz/85 g skein] 1 skein each Espresso(ish) (A), Hot Pink(ish) (B), and Lime(ish) (C) or 50 yds (46 m) each A and B and 65 yds (59 m) C

Tools
• size 7 (4.5 mm) needles

• size H (5 mm) crochet hook

Notions
• Two lengths ribbon measuring 70" (178 cm), shown with ½" (1 cm) width

2-Row Even Stripes

Work 2 rows with A.

Work 2 rows with B.

2 ROW EVEN STRIPES

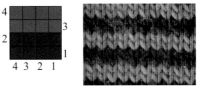

Calf Ruffle

With C, CO 99 sts for top of warmer. Work back and forth in St st as follows:

Work for 1" (2.5 cm), ending after a WS row.

Next Row (RS): *K3tog; rep from * around—33 sts.

Purl 1 row.

Leg

Cut yarn and switch to A. Begin working in 2-Row Even Stripes. Work 2 rows even.

Row 1 (Decrease Row) (RS): K3, k2tog, work to last 5 sts, ssk, k3—2 sts decreased.

Row 2 and all WS rows: Purl.

Row 3: K3, yo, k2tog, work to last 5 sts, ssk, yo, k3.

Rows 5–7: Knit.

Row 9: Work as for Row 3.

Row 11: Knit.

Row 12 (WS): Purl.

Repeat these 12 rows a total of 5 times, then work Row 1 once more—21 sts.

Work 3 rows, ending after 2 rows with A.

Ankle Ruffle

Cut yarn and switch to C.

Work 2 rows in St st.

Increase Row (RS): *Kf&b&f in one stitch; rep from * to end of row—63 sts.

Work back and forth in St st for 1" (2.5 cm). BO all sts.

Finishing

With C, work single crochet (page 17) along both vertical edges of legwarmer. Weave in all loose ends. Fold length of ribbon in half and thread it through bottom two holes of warmer. Crisscross ribbon all the way up, weaving through alternate holes as though for a shoe. Tie a bow at the top.

Chapter 5

Hands

Elbow Mitts

Fingerless mitts that go all the way up the elbow are perfect for warmth and flair. This Fair Isle combination looks great in four or more colors. The chart for this design includes four of the colorwork patterns with some stripes for separation and variety. Cabled ribbing is worked on the cuffs. Shown here in child size.

Size
toddler(child, teen)

Finished Circumference
5½ (6½, 7¼)" [14 (16.5, 18) cm]

Length
10 (12, 14)" [25 (30, 35.5) cm]

Gauge
20 sts and 25 rows per 4" (10 cm) in stockinette stitch

Yarn
- Cascade Yarns 220 Wool [100% wool; 220 yds/201 m per 3.5 oz/100 g skein] 1 skein each #8886 (A), #7814 (B), #9542 (C), and #9463 (D) or 40 (60, 75) yds [36.5 (55, 68.5) m] each A, B, C, & D

Tools
- set of size 7 (4.5 mm) DPNs
- cable needle

Pattern Notes
Choose the size that is slightly smaller than actual hand circumference.

Cabled Rib

(worked over a multiple of 7 (8, 9) sts)

Round 1: *K4, p3 (4, 5); rep from * around.

Round 2: *C4F, p3 (4, 5); rep from * around.

Round 3: *K4, p3 (4, 5); rep from * around.

CABLED RIB

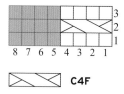

C4F

Arm

With A, CO 28 (32, 36) sts. Divide these sts evenly among 3 DPNs. PM and join to work in the round, being careful not to twist stitches.

Work Rounds 1–3 of Cabled Rib a total of 3 times.

Switch to B and begin working Fair Isle Chart. Repeat chart until piece measures approximately 7 (9, 11)" [18 (23, 28) cm] from CO edge, ending after round 10, 16, or 23. Switch to B and work in the round until piece measures 8 (10, 12)" [20 (25, 30.5) cm] from CO edge.

Set-up for Thumb

Left Hand ONLY:

Next round: K4, k3 (4, 5) with scrap yarn, sl these sts back to LH needle, knit again with working yarn to end of round.

Right Hand ONLY:

Next Round: K to last 7 (8, 9) sts, k3 (4, 5) with scrap yarn, sl these sts back to LH needle, knit again with working yarn to end of round.

Both Hands

Hand

Resume knitting in the round for two more rounds. Switch to A. Work Rounds 1-3 of Cabled Rib 3 times. BO all sts.

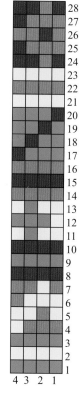

■ A

■ B

■ C

☐ D

Thumb (Make 2)

Place 3 (4, 5) sts on bottom on single DPN, and 2(3, 4) sts on top on second DPN. Carefully pull out scrap yarn for thumb. With B, knit sts from bottom DPN. Use a free DPN to pick up and knit 2 sts in the gap between bottom and top needles, then knit sts from top DPN. Use another DPN to pick up and knit 2 sts on other gap. Place marker for end of round—9 (11, 13) sts.

Knit 3 rounds. Switch to A.

Next Round: K to last 2 sts, k2tog—8 (10, 12) sts.

Next round: *K1, p1, rep from * around.

Work last round once more.

BO all sts in pattern.

Finishing

Weave in all loose ends. Block.

Bracelet Casings

Here are some options for bracelets to play dress up! Each is a quick knit and stitch pattern options vary from colorwork to cables to texture. Casings are worked in the round and seamed around bracelet after bind off. No shaping is involved making it easy to substitute other stitch pattern options.

Textured Casing

Size
one size

Finished Circumference
10¾" (27 cm)

Gauge
24 sts per 4" (10 cm) in Moss Stitch, with yarn held double

Yarn
- Madelinetosh Tosh Merino Light [100% merino; 420 yds/384 m per 3.5 oz/100 g skein] 1 skein Magenta or 90 yds (82 m) fingering weight yarn

Tools
- size 4 (3.5 mm) set of 5 DPNs

Notions
- plastic bangle bracelet

Cabled Casing

Size
one size

Finished Circumference
9" (23 cm)

Gauge
32 sts per 4" (10 cm) in Cable Circles

Yarn
- Madelinetosh Tosh Merino Light [100% merino; 420 yds/384 m per 3.5 oz/100 g skein] 1 skein Tomato or 35 yds (32 m) fingering weight yarn

Tools
- size 2 (2.75 mm) set of 5 DPNs

Notions
- plastic bangle bracelet

Striped Casing

Size
one size

Finished Circumference
10½" (26.5 cm)

Gauge
20 sts per 4" (10 cm) in stockinette stitch

Yarn
- Malabrigo Yarns Merino Worsted [100% merino; 210 yds/192 m per 3.5 oz/100 g skein] 1 skein each Azul Bolita (A) and Molly (B) or 15 yds (14 m) each A & B worsted weight yarn

Tools
- size 7 (4.5 mm) set of 5 DPNs

Notions
- plastic bangle bracelet

CABLED CASING

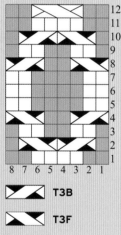

8	7	6	5	4	3	2	1	

12
11
10
9
8
7
6
5
4
3
2
1

▨ **T3B**

▨ **T3F**

Crossing Cable Circles

(worked over a multiple of 8 sts)

Round 1: *P2, k4, p2; rep from * around.

Round 2: *P1, T3B, T3F, p1; rep from * around.

Round 3: *P1, k2, p2, k2, p1; rep from * around.

Round 4: *T3B, p2, T3F; rep from * around.

Rounds 5–7: *K2, p4, k2; rep from * around.

Round 8: *T3F, p2, T3B; rep from * around.

Round 9: *P1, k2, p2, k2, p1; rep from * around.

Round 10: *P1, T3F, T3B, p1; rep from * around.

Round 11: *P2, k4, p2; rep from * around.

Round 12: *P2, C4F, p2; rep from * around.

Cabled Casing

CO 72 sts. Divide sts evenly among 3 DPNs. PM and join to work in the round, being careful not to twist stitches.

Work in Crossing Cable Circles until piece measures twice the width of your bangle bracelet from CO edge, ending after Round 11 of Crossing Cable Circles. Sample bracelet shown is approximately ½" (1 cm) wide, so casing was knit to 1" (2.5 cm) from CO edge. BO all sts.

Slip casing over bracelet and fold in half. Seam CO and BO edges together.

Moss Stitch

Round 1: *K1, p1; rep from * around.

Round 2: Knit.

Round 3: *P1, k1; rep from * around.

Round 4: Knit.

CO 64 sts. Divide sts evenly among 3 DPNs. PM and join to work in the round, being careful not to twist stitches.

Work in Moss Stitch until piece measures twice the width of your bangle bracelet from CO edge, ending after an odd numbered round. Sample bracelet shown is approximately 2¼" (6 cm) wide, so casing was knit to 4½" (11 cm) from CO edge. BO all sts.

Slip casing over bracelet and fold in half. Seam CO and BO edges together.

Vertical Stripes

All Rounds: *With A, k1, with B, k1; rep from * around.

With A, CO 52 sts. Divide sts evenly among 3 DPNs. PM and join to work in the round, being careful not to twist stitches.

Work in Vertical Stripes pattern until piece measures twice the width of your bangle bracelet from CO edge. Sample bracelet shown is approximately 1¼" (3 cm) wide, so casing was knit to 2½" (6 cm) from CO edge. BO all sts.

Slip casing over bracelet and fold in half. Seam CO and BO edges together.

Love Mitts

Picot hems set off these fingerless, thumbless mitts. They are worked back and forth to allow for intarsia and have just enough shaping to help hold them in place on the wrist before flaring out over the hand. If you prefer to work seamlessly, try working the mitts in the round with striping instead. Shown here in child size.

Size
toddler(child, teen)

Finished Circumference
6 (7, 8)" [15 (18, 20) cm]

Length
5½ (6, 6½)" [14 (15, 16.5) cm]

Gauge
20 sts and 26 rows per 4" (10 cm) in stockinette stitch

Yarn
• Patons Classic Wool [100% wool; 210 yds/192 m per 3.5 oz/100 g skein] 1 skein each Orchid (A), Lemongrass (B), and Emerald (C) or 70(90, 115) yds [64 (82, 105) m] A and scraps of B and C.

Tools
• size 7 (4.5 mm) needles

Pattern Notes
Choose the size that is closest to actual hand circumference.

Wrist

With A, CO 23 (27, 31) sts.

Beginning with a WS row, work 3 rows in St st.

Eyelet Row (RS): K1, *yo, k2tog; rep from * to end of row.

Work 5 rows in St st.

Fold work so that eyelet row becomes a picot edge top of cuff.

Joining Row (RS): Join working sts to cast on edge as follows, *with left needle, pick up st from the cast on edge opposite next working st and k2tog with next working st; repeat from * to end of row.

Next Row (WS): P2 (4, 6), pm, p to last 2 (4, 6) sts, pm, p to end.

Heart Intarsia

Note: This section includes work to be done AT THE SAME TIME. Read entire section before beginning.

Increase Row (RS): K1, m1L, work to last st, m1R, K1—2 sts increased.

Work Increase Row every RS row a total of 2 (4, 5) times—31 (35, 41) sts.

AT THE SAME TIME, during first (second, third) Increase Row, begin Heart Intarsia chart over center 19 sts between markers. Work rows 1–18 of Heart Intarsia chart once.

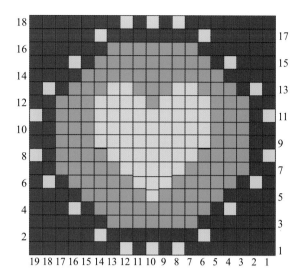

Hand

Work even until mitt measures 5½ (6, 6½)" [14 (15, 16.5) cm] from picot edge.

Work Eyelet Row once more.

Work 5 rows. BO all sts.

Finishing

Fold top edge with WS together and seam to create top picot hem. Seam sides. Weave in all loose ends. Block.

Wrist Cuffs

This pair of unisex cuffs is guaranteed to keep any little boy or girl toasty warm, yet allow hands free for play. Try wearing them on the ankles, too. The cuffs feature just a bit of colorwork and were worked up in the round, asymmetrically. They also knit up well in many other stitch patterns, including the Zigzag or Diagonal. Shown here in child size.

Size
toddler(child, teen)

Width (unstretched)
6¼ (7½, 8½)" [16 (19, 21.5) cm]

Length
7 (7¾, 8½)" [18 (19.5, 21.5) cm]

Gauge
13 sts and 18 rows per 4" (10 cm) in stockinette stitch

Yarn
- Patons Shetland Chunky [75% acrylic, 25% wool; 148 yds/135 m per 3.5 oz/100 g skein] 1 skein each Royal (A) and Leaf Green (B) or 40 (50, 60) yds [36.5 (46, 55) m] each A and B

Tools
- size 9 (5.5 mm) DPNs
- size 10 (6 mm) DPNs
- stitch marker

Pattern Notes
Sample mitts are shown with cuffs and forearm sections reversed in color on the second mitt. Bitty Dots color changes are noted using the mitt with Royal (blue) cuffs and dots.

Bitty Dots

(worked over a multiple of 4 sts)

Round 1: *With B, k1, with A, k1, with B, k2; rep from * around.

Rounds 2–3: With B, knit.

Round 4: *With B, k3, with A, k1; rep from * around.

Rounds 5–6: With B, knit.

BITTY DOTS

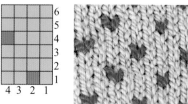

Cuffs

With A and smaller needles, CO 22 (26, 30) sts.

Rib: *K1, p1; rep from * around.

Work in Rib for 1½ (1¾, 2)" [4 (4.5, 5) cm]. Switch to larger needles.

With B, knit one round.

Decrease Round: K1, k2tog, knit to last 3 sts, ssk, k1—2 sts decreased.

Work evenly in Bitty Dots pattern until piece measures 5½ (6, 6½)" [14 (15, 16.5) cm] from CO edge, ending after Round 2 or Round 5.

Work Decrease Round once more—18 (22, 26) sts. Cut B. Switch to smaller needles.

With A, knit one round. Work in Rib for 1½ (1¾, 2)" [4 (4.5, 5) cm]. BO all sts.

Finishing

Weave in all loose ends. Block.

Ruffled Cufflets

These frilly feminine mitts coordinate with the ruffled capelet—ideal for your modern girly-girl. Cufflets add panache to a spring dress or an edgy ensemble. They are worked from the wrist to the hand in the round. Shown here in child size.

Size
toddler (child, teen)

Finished Circumference
6¼ (7, 8¼)" [16 (18, 21) cm]

Length
5 (5½, 6)" [12.5 (14, 15) cm]

Gauge
26 sts and 34 rows per 4" (10 cm) in stockinette stitch

Yarn
• Shibui Knits Sock [100% merino; 191 yds/175 m per 1.8 oz/50 g skein] 1 skein Periwinkle or 110 (130, 170) yds [100.5 (119, 155) m]

Tools
• size 4 (3.5 mm) DPNs

Notions
• Marsha Neal Studios Handpainted Silky Ribbon in #93 Grey Blue or 1 yd (1 m) ribbon

Pattern Notes
Cuffs designed to be slightly loose on the hand. Choose the size that is larger than actual hand circumference.

Cufflet (Make 2)

CO 81 (90, 108) sts. Divide sts evenly among 3 DPNs. PM and join to work in the round, being careful not to twist stitches. Knit for 1" (2.5 cm).

Decrease Round: *K3tog; rep from * around—27 (30, 36) sts.

Knit 3 rounds.

Eyelet Round: *yo twice, k2tog, k2, yo twice, k2tog, k3 (4, 6); rep from * around.

Knit 3 rounds, dropping first yo of each eyelet on first round.

Hand

Increase Round: *K2, m1; rep from * to last 1 (0, 0) st, knit to end—40 (45, 54) sts.

Knit in the round until cufflet measures 1½ (2, 2½)" [4 (5, 6) cm] from eyelet round.

Set-up for Thumb: K4 (5, 6) with scrap yarn, sl these sts back to LH needle, knit again with working yarn.

Resume knitting in the round for one more inch.

Decrease Round: *K2tog; rep from * to last 0 (1, 0) st, knit to end—20 (23, 27) sts.

Knit 3 rounds.

Increase Round: *Kf&b&f in one stitch; rep from * around—60 (69, 81) sts.

Knit in the round for 1" (2.5 cm).

BO all sts.

Thumb

Place 4 (5, 6) sts on bottom on single DPN, and 3 (4, 5) sts on top on second DPN. Carefully pull out scrap yarn for thumb. Knit across sts on bottom DPN. Use free DPN to pick up and knit 2 sts in the gap between bottom and top needles, then knit sts from top DPN. Use another DPN to pick up and knit 2 sts on other gap. PM for end of round—11 (13, 15) sts. Knit 6 rounds. BO all sts.

Finishing

Weave in all loose ends. Cut ribbon in half to make two strands, each 18" (46 cm) long. Thread ribbon in and out of eyelets, keeping ribbon on RS of mitt over longer segments.

Chapter 6

Toes

Striped Ankle Socks

These easy ankle socks knit up quickly. They are super stretchy thanks to the textured striping and are sure to last a long time. The socks are worked toe-up with short rows only at the heel. Shown here in tween size.

Size
toddler (child, tween)

Foot Circumference
5½ (6, 6½, 7)" [14 (15, 16.5, 18) cm]

Gauge
20 sts and 27 rows per 4" (10 cm) in stockinette stitch

Yarn
• Berroco Comfort [50% superfine nylon, 50% superfine acrylic; 210 yds/193 m per 3.5 oz/100 g skein] 1 skein each Kidz Orange (A), Goldenrod (B), and Primary Red (C) or 30 (40, 50, 55) yds [27 (36.5, 46, 50) m] A and 25 (35, 40, 50) yds [23 (32, 36.5, 46) m] each B and C

Tools
• size 7 (4.5 mm) DPNs
• size 8 (5 mm) DPNs
• stitch marker

Pattern Notes
Pattern is written based on the sample shown with orange heel and toe. Sock with red heel and toe uses same striping pattern with the following color assignments: Primary Red (A), Kidz Orange (B), and Goldenrod (C).

Textured Stripe Pattern

Round 1: With B, purl.

Rounds 2–3: With B, knit.

Round 4: With C, purl.

Rounds 5–6: With C, knit.

Round 7: With A, purl.

Rounds 8–9: With A, knit.

Toe

With A and a single larger DPN, CO 9 (10, 11, 12) sts. *With 2 more DPNs, slip first stitch to first DPN and second stitch to second DPN. Repeat from * until there are 5 (5, 6, 6) sts on the first dpn and 4 (5, 5, 6) sts on the second. PM and join to work in the round. Knit 1 round, beginning with a third DPN and adding a fourth as you knit around. Arrange the stitches on three needles and work with a fourth.

First Increase Round: *K1, m1; rep from * around—18 (20, 22, 24) sts.

Knit 1 round.

Second Increase Round: *K2, m1; rep from * around—27 (30, 33, 36) sts.

Knit 3 rounds.

Work Rounds 1–9 of Textured Stripe pattern 3 (4, 5, 6) times, then work Rounds 1–6 once more. Sock measures about 4½ (6, 6½, 7)" [11 (15, 16.5, 18) cm] from CO of toe. Stretch sock gently to measure the length.

Heel

With A, knit to last 6 (7, 8, 9) sts.

Short rows (W&T, page 17) for the heel will be worked over the next 12 (14, 16, 18) sts. Leave end-of-round marker in place, slipping it back and forth during the short rows.

Short Rows 1–2: K12 (14, 16, 18), W&T, p12 (14, 16, 18), W&T.

Short Rows 3–4: Knit to 1 st before wrapped st, W&T, purl to 1 st before wrapped st, W&T.

Work Short Rows 3–4 a total of 3 (4, 5, 5) times—6 (6, 6, 8) sts remain in between wrapped sts.

Short Rows 1–2: Knit to first wrapped st, knit wrapped st with wrap, W&T, sl 1, purl to first wrapped st, purl wrapped st with wrap, W&T.

Short Rows 3–4: Sl 1, knit to first double-wrapped st, knit double-wrapped st with both wraps, W&T, sl 1, purl to first double wrapped st, purl double-wrapped st with both wraps, W&T.

Work Short Rows 3–4 a total of 3 (4, 5, 5) times—1 double wrapped st remains on each end.

Next Row: Sl 1, knit to double-wrapped st, knit double-wrapped st with both wraps, DO NOT TURN. Resume working in the round.

Work Rounds 1–6 of Textured Stripe Pattern, working remaining double-wrapped st with both wraps on first round and decreasing 1 (0, 1, 0) st on last round—26 (30, 32, 36) sts. Cut B and C.

Switch to A and smaller needles. Purl 1 round.

Rib: *K1, p1; rep from * around.

Work 2 rounds in Rib.

BO all stitches using a stretchy bind-off method such as Jeny's Surprisingly Stretchy Bind-Off (page 17).

Finishing

Weave in all loose ends. Block.

Tiered Ruffle Socks

Here are fanciful knee highs to wear with a miniskirt and Mary Janes or a tunic and ankle booties! These socks are accented with stripes, stranded colorwork, and three layers of ruffles. They are knit toe-up with short-row shaping at both heel and toe. Shown here in child size.

Size
toddler (child, teen)

Foot Circumference
4½ (5¾, 6½)" [11 (14.5, 16.5) cm]

Foot Length
6 (7, 8)" [15 (18, 20) cm]

Gauge
22 sts and 28 rows per 4" (10 cm) in stockinette stitch

Yarn
• Skacel Hikoo Simplicity [55% merino, 28% acrylic, 17% nylon; 117 yds/107 m per 1.8 oz/50 g skein] 1 skein each #006 (A), #010 (B), #033 (C), and #034 (D) or 40 (60, 75) yds [36.5 (55, 68.5) m] each A and C and 60 (85, 105) yds [55 (78, 96) m] each B and D in DK weight yarn

Tools
• size 4 (3.5 mm) DPNs

• size 5 (3.75 mm) DPNs

• size F (3.75 mm) crochet hook

Pattern Notes
Circumference is stretchy and sized with negative ease, measurement should be smaller than recipient.

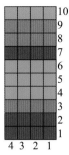

Kooky Stripes

Rounds 1–2: Knit in C.

Round 3: Knit in D.

Rounds 4–6: Knit in B.

Round 7: Knit in C.

Rounds 8–9: Knit in D.

Round 10: Knit in B.

Flower & Dot

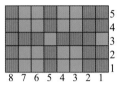

(worked over a multiple of 8 sts)

Rounds 1–2: *With A, k2, [with B, k2, with A, k1] twice; rep from * to end.

Round 3: *With B, k1, with A, k3; rep from * to end.

Rounds 4–5: * With A, k2, [with B, k2, with A, k1] twice; rep from * to end.

Ruffle Cuffs

Note: Make 3 cuffs for each sock, one each in B, C, & D.

With larger DPNs, CO 72 (96, 108) sts. PM and join to work in the round, being careful not to twist sts. Knit 4 rounds.

Decrease Round: *K3tog; rep from * around—24 (32, 36) sts.

Slip to spare DPNs or circular needles. Set Aside.

Toe

With scrap yarn and crochet hook, provisionally CO 12 (16, 18) sts onto larger DPN. With A, purl 1 WS row.

Work toe using Short Rows (W&T, page 17) as follows:

Short Rows 1–2: Knit to last st, W&T, purl to last st, W&T.

Short Rows 3–4: Knit to 1 st before wrapped st, W&T, purl to 1 st before wrapped st, W&T.

Work Short Rows 3–4 a total of 4 times—4 (8, 10) sts remain unwrapped.

Note: The following short rows result in stitches that are double wrapped. On subsequent rows, make

sure to pick up BOTH wraps when knitting them with the wrapped st.

Short Rows 1–2: Knit to first wrapped st, knit wrapped st together with wrap, W&T, sl 1, purl to first wrapped st, purl wrapped st together with wrap, W&T.

Short Rows 3–4: Sl 1, knit to first double-wrapped st, knit double-wrapped st together with wraps, W&T, sl 1, purl to first double wrapped st, purl double-wrapped st together with wraps, W&T.

Work Short Rows 3–4 a total of 3 times, one double-wrapped st remains at each end.

Next Row: Sl 1, knit to double-wrapped st, knit double-wrapped st together with wraps, DO NOT TURN.

Remove provisional CO and place 12 (16, 18) sts on needles, ready to work—24 (32, 36) sts.

PM and join to work in the round, work across provisionally CO sts, k16, knit to end of round, working remaining wraps together with wrapped st—36 sts.

Knit 1 round. Cut yarn, leaving a long tail to weave in.

With B, knit 1 round.

Work even in Kooky Stripes until sock measures 4½ (6, 7¼)" [11 (15, 18) cm] from toe.

Heel

Heel will be worked back and forth over last 12 (16, 18) sts.

K12 (16, 18). Switch to A.

Short Rows 1–2: K11 (15, 17), W&T, p10 (14, 16), W&T.

Short Rows 3–4: Knit to 1 st before wrapped st, W&T, purl to 1 st before wrapped st, W&T.

Work Short Rows 3–4 a total of 4 times—4 (8, 10) sts remain unwrapped.

Note: The following short rows result in stitches that are double wrapped. On subsequent rows, make sure to pick up BOTH wraps when knitting them with the wrapped st.

Short Rows 1–2: Knit to first wrapped st, knit wrapped st together with wrap, W&T, sl 1, purl to first wrapped st, purl wrapped st together with wrap, W&T.

Short Rows 3–4: Sl 1, knit to first double-wrapped st, knit double-wrapped st together with wraps, W&T, sl 1, purl to first double-wrapped st, purl double-wrapped st together with wraps, W&T.

Work Short Rows 3–4 a total of 3 times, one double-wrapped st remains at end of each row.

Next Row: Sl 1, knit to double-wrapped st, k double-wrapped st together with wrap. DO NOT TURN.

Resume working in the round in Kooky Stripes. Pick up 1 st at the end of current row, sm, pick up another st, k12 (16, 18), pick up 2 sts before picking up wraps and working wrapped st as at other end of heel, knit to end of row—28 (36, 40) sts.

Next round: K2tog, k10 (14, 16), ssk, k2tog, k to last 2 sts, ssk—24 (32, 36) sts.

Resume working Kooky Stripes pattern. Work even until leg measures 6 (7, 8)" [15 (18, 20) cm] from bottom of heel. Cut B and C, switch to D. Knit 3 rounds.

Work Flower and Dot Chart over next 5 rounds.

Work 7 more rounds in D. Cut yarn.

Switch to A. Pick up first ruffle.

Slip ruffle onto top so that working needles are bottom layer with ruffle needles layered on top.

Joining Round: *K2tog with one st from working needle and one st from ruffle layer; rep from * around.

Knit 4 rounds.

Repeat Joining Round with second ruffle.

Knit 4 rounds.

Repeat Joining Round with third ruffle.

Switch to smaller DPNs and work in a 1x1 rib for 5 rounds.

BO all sts with Jeny's Surprisingly Stretchy Bind-off (page 17).

Finishing

Weave in all loose ends. Block.

Funky Fair Isle Socks

Four colors are incorporated into this fingering weight design. These socks are worked toe-up with a contrasting toe, foot, and heel, then finished with a calf-length leg featuring Fair Isle colorwork. Use the provided chart, or pick your own stitch-pattern combination from the dictionary on pages 20–24. Shown here in child size.

Size
toddler (child, teen)

Foot Circumference
4½ (5¾, 6¾)" [11 (14.5, 17) cm]

Foot Length: 6 (7, 8)" [15 (18, 20) cm]

Gauge
28 sts and 30 rows per 4" (10 cm) in stockinette stitch

Yarn
- Spud & Chloë Fine [80% superwash wool, 20% silk; 248 yds/227 m per 2.3 oz/65 g skein] 1 skein each Hippo (A), Wildberries (B), Goldfish (C), and Lizard (D) or 30 (45, 60) yds [27 (41, 55) m] each A, B, and D and 55 (90, 130) yds [50 (82, 119) m] C fingering weight yarn

Tools
- size 2 (2.75 mm) DPNs
- size 3 (3.25 mm) DPNs
- size D (3.25 mm) crochet hook

Pattern Notes
Circumference is stretchy and sized with negative ease; measurement should be smaller than recipient.

Toe

With scrap yarn and crochet hook, provisionally CO 16 (20, 24) sts to larger DPN.

With A, purl 1 WS row.

Work short rows (W&T, page 17) to shape toe as follows:

Short Rows 1–2: Knit to last st, W&T, purl to last st, W&T.

Short Rows 3–4: Knit to 1 st before wrapped st, W&T, purl to 1 st before wrapped st, W&T.

Work Short Rows 3–4 a total of 4 (5, 6) times—6 (8, 10) sts remain unwrapped.

Note: The following short rows result in stitches that are double wrapped. On subsequent rows, make sure to pick up BOTH wraps when knitting them with the wrapped st.

Short Rows 1–2: Knit to first wrapped st, knit wrapped st together with wrap, W&T, sl 1, purl to first wrapped st, purl wrapped st together with wrap, W&T.

Short Rows 3–4: Sl 1, knit to first double-wrapped st, knit double-wrapped st together with both wraps, W&T, sl 1, purl to first double-wrapped st, purl double-wrapped st together with both wraps, W&T.

Work Short Rows 3–4 a total of 3 (4, 5) times—one double-wrapped st remains at end of each row.

Next Row (RS): Sl 1, knit to double-wrapped st, knit double-wrapped st, DO NOT TURN. Cut yarn.

Remove provisional CO and place 16 (20, 24) sts on needles, ready to work—32 (40, 48) sts.

With B, knit 2 rounds, working wraps together with double-wrapped st on first round.

Cut yarn.

With C, work even until sock measures 4½ (5½, 6½)" [11 (14, 16.5) cm] from toe or about 1½" (4 cm) less than desired length. Do not cut yarn.

With B, knit 2 rounds. Do not cut yarn.

Heel

With D, work heel back and forth over first 16 (20, 24) sts as follows:

Short Rows 1–2: K15 (19, 23), W&T, p14 (18, 22), W&T.

Short Rows 3–4: Knit to 1 st before wrapped st, W&T, purl to 1 st before wrapped st, W&T.

Work Short Rows 3–4 a total of 4 (5, 6) times—6 (8, 10) sts remain unwrapped.

Note: The following short rows result in stitches that are double wrapped. On subsequent rows, make sure to pick up BOTH wraps when knitting them with the wrapped st.

Short Rows 1–2: Knit to first wrapped st, knit wrapped st together with wrap, W&T, sl 1, purl to first wrapped st, purl wrapped st together with wrap, W&T.

Short Rows 3–4: Sl 1, knit to first double-wrapped st, knit double-wrapped st together with both wraps, W&T, sl 1, purl to first double-wrapped st, purl double-wrapped st together with both wraps, W&T.

Work Short Rows 15–16 a total of 3 (4, 5) times, one double-wrapped st remains at end of each row.

Next Row: Sl 1, knit to double-wrapped st, knit double-wrapped st together with both wraps. DO NOT TURN.

Switch to B and resume working in the round. Pick up 1 st at the end of current row, sm, pick up another st, k16 (20, 24), pick up 2 sts before picking up wraps and working wrapped st as at other end of heel, knit to end of row—36 (44, 52) sts.

Next round: K2tog, k14 (18, 22), ssk, k2tog, knit to last 2 sts, ssk—32 (40, 48) sts.

Begin working in Funky Fair Isle.

Work even in pattern until sock measures 6½ (7½, 8½)" [16.5 (19, 21.5) cm] from turn of heel, ending after working any solid color round.

Cut yarn for A, C, and D and switch to B.

Cuff

Knit 1 round. Switch to smaller needles.

Ribbing: *P3, k1; rep from * around.

Work in Ribbing until cuff measures 1½" (4 cm).

BO all sts with Jeny's Surprisingly Stretchy Bind-off (page 17).

Finishing

Weave in all loose ends. Block.

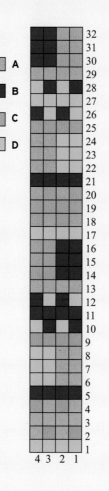

Stranded Socks

These socks knit toe-up, in the round with short-row shaping at the heel and turn of the ankle. They are shown with sweet Hearts, but you can try them in Polka Dots, too. They also work perfectly with the Spiral and Flower & Dot colorwork options! Shown here in child size.

Size
toddler (child, teen)

Foot Circumference
4½ (5¾, 6¾)" [11 (14.5, 17) cm]

Foot Length
6 (7, 8)" [15 (18, 20) cm]

Gauge
28 sts and 37 rows per 4" (10 cm) in stockinette stitch

Yarn
- Anzula Dreamy [75% merino, 15% cashmere, 10% silk; 385 yds/352 m per 4.1 oz/115 g skein] 1 skein each Curry (A) and Ballerina (B) or 40 (60, 80) yds [36.5 (55, 73) m] A and 65 (100, 130) yds [59 (91, 119) m] B

Tools
- size 3 (3.25 mm) DPNs
- size D (3.25 mm) crochet hook

Pattern Notes
Circumference is stretchy and sized with negative ease; measurement should be smaller than recipient.

HEARTS

18 17 16 15 14 13 12 11 10 9 8 7 6 5 4 3 2 1

8 7 6 5 4 3 2 1

POLKA DOTS

18 17 16 15 14 13 12 11 10 9 8 7 6 5 4 3 2 1

8 7 6 5 4 3 2 1

Toe

With scrap yarn and crochet hook, provisionally CO 16 (20, 24) sts. With A, purl 1 WS row. Work short rows (W&T, page 17) as follows:

Short Rows 1–2: Knit to last st, W&T, purl to last st, W&T.

Short Rows 3–4: Knit to one st before wrapped st, W&T, purl to one st before wrapped st, W&T.

Work Short Rows 3–4 a total of 4 (5, 6) times—6 (8, 10) remain between wrapped sts.

Short Rows 1–2: Knit to first wrapped st, knit wrapped st with wrap, W&T, sl 1, purl to first wrapped st, purl wrapped st with wrap, W&T.

Short Rows 3–4: Sl 1, knit to first double-wrapped st, knit double-wrapped st with both wraps, W&T, sl 1, purl to first double-wrapped st, purl double-wrapped st with both wraps, W&T.

Work Short Rows 3–4 a total of 3 (4, 5) times—one double-wrapped st remains at end of each row.

Next Row: Sl 1, knit to double-wrapped st, knit double-wrapped st with both wraps, DO NOT TURN.

Remove provisional CO and place 16 (20, 24) sts on needles, ready to work in the round—32 (40, 48) sts.

Pick up and knit 1 st at the end of current row, pm and join to work in the round, pick up and knit 1 st at beginning of provisionally CO sts, k16 (20, 24), pick up and knit one st at end of provisionally CO sts, pick up and knit 1 st at beginning of original set of sts, knit double-wrapped st with both wraps, knit to end of round—36 (44, 52) sts. Knit 1 round.

Cut yarn. Switch to B.

Next round: K2tog, k16 (18, 20), ssk, k2tog, k to last 2 sts, ssk—32 (40, 48) sts.

Work in St st until sock measures 4½ (6, 7¼)" [11 (15, 18) cm] from tip of toe.

Heel

Knit 16 (20, 24), then work heel over remaining 16 (20, 24) sts as follows:

Short Rows 1–2: With A, k15 (19, 23), W&T, p14 (18, 22), W&T.

Short Rows 3–4: Knit to one st before wrapped st, W&T, purl to one st before wrapped st, W&T.

Work Short Rows 3–4 a total of 4 (5, 6) times—6 (8, 10) remain between wrapped sts.

Short Rows 1–2: Knit to first wrapped st, knit wrapped st with wrap, W&T, sl 1, purl to first wrapped st, purl wrapped st with wrap, W&T.

Short Rows 3–4: Sl 1, knit to first double-wrapped st, knit double-wrapped st with both wraps, W&T, sl 1, purl to first double-wrapped st, purl double-wrapped st with both wraps, W&T.

Work Short Rows 3–4 a total of 3 (4, 5) times, one double-wrapped st remains at each end.

Next Row: Sl 1, knit to double-wrapped st, knit double-wrapped st with both wraps, DO NOT TURN. Cut A. Resume working in the round.

With B, knit 2 rounds, working remaining double-wrapped st with both wraps.

Leg

Work Rounds 1–18 of Polka Dots or Heart chart.

Size Child ONLY: Work Rounds 1–10 once more.

Size Teen ONLY: Work full Chart once more.

ALL SIZES: Cut B.

Cuff

With A, knit 1 round.

Crossover Round: *X2, rep from * around.

Knit 1 round.

Repeat the last two rounds a total of 5 times.

BO all sts with Jeny's Surprisingly Stretchy Bind-off (page 17).

Finishing

Weave in all loose ends. Block.

★ Yarn and Notion Sources

Anzula
559-457-9957
www.anzula.com

AskCheese Wooden Buttons
www.etsy.com/shop/askcheese

Berroco, Inc.
401-769-1212
www.berroco.com

Blue Sky Alpacas
763-753-5815
888-460-8862
www.blueskyalpacas.com

Caron
888-368-8401
www.caron.com

Cascade Yarns
800-548-1048
www.cascadeyarns.com

Ewe Ewe Yarns
760-933-8393
www.eweewe.com

Heyday Handmade
www.etsy.com/shop/heydayhandmade

Lion Brand
800-258-YARN (9276)
www.lionbrand.com

Lorna's Laces
773-935-3803
www.lornaslaces.net

Madelinetosh
817-249-3066
www.madelinetosh.com

Malabrigo
786-866-6187
www.malabrigoyarn.com

Marsha Neal Studio, LLC
www.MarshaNealStudio.com

Patons
1-888-368-8401
www.patonsyarns.com

Rowan
800-445-9276
www.knitrowan.com

Shibui Knits
503-595-5898
www.shibuiknits.com

Skacel Collection, Inc
800-255-1278
www.skacelknitting.com

Spud & Chloë
888-460-8862
www.spudandchloe.com

✭ About the Author

Kate Oates is the designer for Tot Toppers, a children's line of hats and garments, and When I Grow Up, an adult pattern line in a modern, classic style. She enjoys designing hats and garments for babies and children in particular, and her projects reflect a whimsical spirit. Kate strives to add specifically to the growing body of knits for boys, as she has three of her own! You can find her patterns at your local yarn store or online. She also does freelance work for a variety of publications.

In her nonknitting life, Kate holds a PhD in Political Science from the University of Florida. She lives in South Carolina with her family, which includes her husband, Ryan, children Jesse, Charlie, and Oliver (very handsome Tot Topper's models), and beloved dogs Cooper and Lou. You might also see the Oates clan at a Clemson football game. Go Tigers!

Index